Gypsy Messenger

Gypsy Messenger

poems by Marijan Megla
photographs by Sima Khorrami

slipstream

Slipstream Books

A SLIPSTREAM BOOK

Published by: Slipstream (River) Books
an imprint of The Books Collective
214-21, 10405 Jasper Avenue
Edmonton, Alberta, Canada T5J 3S2
river@bookscollective.com

The Books Collective acknowledges the support of the Canada Council for the Arts for our publishing programme. We also acknowledge the assistance of the Edmonton Arts Council.

Sima Khorrami wishes to acknowledge the assistance of the Alberta Foundation for the Arts, the Canada Council, Kodak Canada and Celebration of Women in the Arts for support during the pursuit of her Romany photography project, from which are drawn the images in this book.

Editor for the press: Candas Jane Dorsey.
Outside editor: Amber Hayward.
Cover design: Gerry Dotto.
Cover and inside photographs: Sima Khorrami.
Interior typeset by Jason Bartletti in Adobe's *ITC Officina Serif* and *ITC Officina Sans* with headings in Image Club's *Ultra Condensed Serif*.
Printed on Luna Matte 70lb Text with a Cornwall C1S 10pt cover by Priority Printing, Edmonton.
Our thanks for divers services to Kim Lundquist, T.J. Anderson, Miki Andrejevic and Peter Harris.

National Library of Canada Cataloguing in Publication Data

Megla, Marijan.
Gypsy messenger

ISBN 1-895836-82-4

1. Gypsies – Pictorial works.
I. Khorrami, Sima. II. Title.
PS8576.E34G96 2001 C811'.54 C2001-911653-5
PR9199.3.M42488G96 2001

Gypsy messengers—Gipsi mesingers

On a lonely mountain pass
forgotten by people and beasts
known only to poor men
who passed here in their chains
accused by the law,
of stirring up revolution
now long gone to gulags in Siberia
or vanished from this world
leaving only scratched names
in heavy wooden church benches
where they prayed for the last time
on European soil, praying
that the chains don't cut their legs
unworthy shoes should last the trip,
that the clothes they have
protect them from the bitter cold
on the journey.
Hoping that in time when the Mass is finished
and the long column is slowly built
with the always-present guards swearing
pushing them into groups
they could talk to gypsies
who waited in the forest clearing
with their wagons, ready to move
to leave the message for those at home
I am still alive, passing through the Urals.
Yelling over and over their names
and the towns from which they were taken
mixing their voices with hundreds of others
promising the gypsies plenty of food
given to them by those who stayed home
waiting for some message.
Knowing that hunger lurks
in homes they left.
Then they slowly walk the road
unsure if the gypsies got their news
or will remember names, towns...streets
or are simply willing to go so far.
Soon their heads are turned back no more
slowly they walk, to the sound of chains
swearing of drunken guards
leaving their destiny to God and the gypsies
hoping that their mothers
got the news, that they were still alive
when passing through the Urals.

An lonli maunten pes
fergoten from pipel and bist
non onli tu pur men
det pest hir in dei cheins
ekjust from lo,
tu stir de revolushen
nau long gon, for gulaks in Sibiria
or venisht from des vorld
living onli skrecht neims
in hevi vuden chrch benks
ver dei prei for letzt taim
an Evropa soil, preing
det cheins dont kat dei legs
anvurdi chus hold de trip,
det klos vich dei hev
protekt dem from biter kold,
an des gerni.
Hoping det in taim ven mes is finished
and long kolon is sloli bildet
vit olveis present gards sverin
pushing dem in grups
dei kud tok tu gipsis
det veidet in des forest kliring
vit dei chergas, redi tu muv
tu liv de mesich, for dos et hom
I am stil a laiv, ven pesing Ural.
Jaling over and over dei neims
and tauns from vich dei ver teken
miksing dei voisis vit handert of aders
promising gipsis plenti of fud
given tu dem from dem det stei hom
an veid an sam mesich.
Noing det hanger lrt
in homs dei left
Den dei sloli vok de rod
anshor if gipsis god dei njus
remember neims, tauns...strits
or simpli viling tu go so far.
Sun dei heds trnt bek, no mor
sloli dei vok, in saund of cheins
svering of drank gards
living god, and gipsis dei destinis
hoping det dei maders
god de njues, dei are stil a laiv
ven pesing Ural.

Crazy Mara—Krezi Mara

In a small village	In a smol vileg
where a dozen shacks	ver dasent sheks
crawl on the sandy beach	krol an sendi bich
of a river	of a river
which with only a vague promise of rushing water	vich onli veg promis of rashing vota
stays dry most of the year	kip drai, mosli taim of a jer,
deep in the forest	dip in de forest
squatting on the land of the Gajas,	an Gajas skvotert lend,
she lives alone	shi liv alon
abandoned by men	abendet from men
who left her, tired of her crazy behaviour	det left her, taet of her kresi behevju
tired of her nightmares when she screamed,	taet of her naitmers ven shi skrimt,
after she found her way back from the camp	after she faund bek from kemp
skinny like bamboo	skini laik banbu
when the war ended.	ven vor endet.
She never took a bath	Shi never tuket bet
in the river, like the other women did	in de river, laik ader fimels
before they crushed sweet-smelling flowers	befor dei smir smeli flauers
on their naked skin, and she	in dei neket skin, and her
shivered in water just ankle-deep.	shivering ven her enkels vas kaveret vit vota
But when the river surprised her,	Bad ven river soprais her
and rose to flood the town	and ros tu flad de taun
she screamed, terrified,	shi skrimed terofaid,
staying in her dwelling	steing in her dveling
remembering the night in the Budapest jail	remembering, de nait in Budapeast gel
when bombing burst the water pipe	ven bombing bast de voter paip
which flooded the basement	vich fladet besment
where she was chained	ver shi vos cheint
and for hours, rats that swam around her	and for auers, reds det svim tu her
ate from her naked body.	it from her neket bodi.

Croatia

Crazy *primash* Farkashi—Krezi *primash* Farkashi

On early summer nights	In erli samer nait
when storks in their nests	ven storks in dei nest
on power poles	an pauer pols
around the streets	a raund de strits
quiet down	kvaet daun
when old folks	ven old foks
after heavy suppers	after hevi sapers
settle down on their benches	setel daun in dei benches
beside big property doors	besaid big properti dors
talking over past times	toking over pest taims
in the little cemetery	an litel simenteri
beside a church	bisaid a chrch
in the middle of town	in midel of taun
crazy gypsy Farkashi, the fiddler,	krezi gipsi Farkashi ... de primash
lights a candle, and grieves for his daughter	laitet kendel, an grev of his doter
his only child.	his onli chaild.
Soon there is music	Sun der bi a mjuzik
from his violin	from his vajolin
that made him famous once	det mek him femos vans
filling the space	filing spes
in between the warm roofs	in betvin vorm rufs
and the coming night.	and kaming nait.
For many years now	For meni jers nau
the old people	de old pipel
in winter's long evenings	in vinters long ivnings
have told the sad story	telin des sed stori
turning the primash's life tragedy	trning primash laif tragedi
into the town's legend.	in tu tauns legend.
It was his daughter's birthday	It vos his doter brsdei,
they say, sighing always,	dei sei, ... sajing olveis
and only fourteen years	and onli fortint
in her short, sickly life.	in her short sikli laif.
After she lost her mother	After shi lost her mader,
she caught the coughing sickness, that never left.	shi kech kofing, ... det never left
Instead of keeping her happy	Insted tu kip her hepi
he walked out	hi vok aut
to play at a Gaja's wedding	tu plei an Gajas veding
somewhere in another town.	samver in ader taun.

Next day when they found the *primash*	Neks dei ven dei faun de primash
his daughter was dead.	his doter vos ded
Bad conscience struck the man	Bed konches strak de men
stuck to his soul	stak tu his sol
never leaving him alone.	never livin him alon.
In the years that had since passed	Iven jers are nau pest
hardly anybody has seen	hardli enibadi so
his loner's face.	his loners fes.
People say he is grey now	Pipel teling, ... hi is grei nau
his grey moustache and long hair	his grei mustash and long her
trailing beside hin	treiling besaid him
over flowery meadows.	over flaueri medovs.
Slim as a bony ghost	Slim laik boni gost
with hardly any clothes, he walks	vit hardli eni klos, ... hi voks
hiding in fields	Haiding in filds
or willow bushes	or vilo bushes
beside lazy streams	besaid lezi strims
taking only candles	teking onli kendels
left by Gajas	left from Gajas
on his child's grave.	an his chailds grev.
In the early morning	In erli morning
when the last toothless grannies	ven letzt tutlos grenis
feel the need to crawl into their beds	filet nid, tu krol, in dei beds
leaving their benches	living dei benches
to the night,	tu nait,
crazy Farkashi, the *primash*,	krezi Farkashi, ... de primash
ignored by the dogs	ignort from de dogs
silently walks the streets	sailend vok de strits
taking only his violin	teking onli his vajolin
his sad heart	sed hart
to hide through the day	tu haid tru de dei
in our fields,	in auer filds,
only to return	onli tu retrn
by the nightfall	bai de nait fol
to play for his neglected child.	tu plei for his negolektet chaild.

Hungary

Fortune teller—Fjucher telerin

O *doña* Maria	O donja Maria
wise *gitana*	vaiz gitana
where is my promised love	ver iz mai promis lav
which you saw in my palm	vich ju soet, in mai po
wait a little, wait a lot	veide litel,...veide lat
one day will come my promised luck	van dei vil kam mai promis lak
O *doña* Maria	O donja Maria
wise *gitana*	vaiz gitana
my prime is quickly	mai praim is kvikli
passing me by	pesing mi bai
wait a little,...wait a lot	veide litel,...veide lat
one day will come my promised luck.	van dei vil kam mai promis lak

Spain

Orsari Bear—Orsari Ber

Trrr....rum....ta, ta	Trrr....rum....ta, ta
Round and round	Raund and raund
with muzzle, long chain ... and empty stomach	vit de mazel, long chein ....an emti stamak
on the boring beat of a drum,	an boring bit of a drom
on his light feet,	an his letct fit
taller than the men in that crowd,	toler den eni men in det kraud
he plays drunken husband	plei dranken hasbent
lazy wife, clumsy son,	lezi vaif ....klamsi san
wrestling with all the macho boys	resling vit ol macho bois
just so they can impress their sweethearts	gast tu inpres dei svitharts
in the town.	in des taun.
Around his iron cage	Eraund his aern keig
on an old gypsy wagon,	an old gipsi cherga
teasing tired skinny horses	tising taet skini horsis
still in harness	stil in harnes.
to delight little children	tu delait of lital children
hopping on the shoulders of their older folks	hoping an sholders, of dei older foks
once a year	vans a jer
in the big market square.	an big market skver.
Round and round	Raund and raund
he turns	hi trn
from one to the other little city	from van tu di ader litel siti
a never-ending circus tour	an never ending cirkus tur
to fill the always-empty family coffers.	tu fil olveis emti femili kofin.
Remembering his free days	Remembering, his fri deis
in the wild Balkan mountains	in vaild maunteins of Bolkan
before the gypsy took him	befor dei gipsi tek him
in muzzle and chain	in mazel and chein
away from his home.	evei from his hom.

Turkey

Vida, the coal deliverer—Vida de kol deliverer

Clip, clop, clip, clop	klip, klap, klip, klap
a hungry horse's hooves	a hangri hors hufs
beat the cobbled streets of a	bit de kabel strits of a
north Croatian county	nort Croeshen caunti
pulling a little gypsy wagon	puling litel gipsi vegen
full of rough broken coal	fol of raf broken kol
with Vida, sitting on a blanket	vit Vida, siting an de blanket
shaking with his load	sheking vit his lod
happily greeting people by their names	hepili griting pipel bai dei neims
hoping that they order a wagon of coal	hoping det dei order a vegen of kol
before winter chokes the city	befor vinter chok det siti.
Clip, clop, clip, clop	klip klap klip klap
on the first day of autumn	an frst kold dei of a otom
that has wrapped the city in fog	det reped Siti in de fog
when the cheap coal has finally arrived,	ven chip kol faineli eraivt
in open wagons	in open vegens
at the old German station	an old kaiser steishen
in the middle of the old city	in mitel of a old siti.
early in the morning	ver erli in de moning
a line is formed	lain is formt
of coal deliverers	from kol deliverer
loading bigger boulders by hand	vit hend biger bolder a lodet
so that customers don't complain	so det kastim dont konplein
they are getting only coal dust	geding onli kol dast
Steadily calming down his horse,	stedili kaming daun his hors
Vida shovels smaller pieces	Vida shavelt smoler pisis
to make a load.	tu mek a lod.
Then in a hurry, moves on to deliver	Den in heri, muv on tu deliver
hoping that the clients are home	hoping det klaent is hom
have money to pay him	hev de mani tu pei him
and don't cheat him because he is a gypsy.	or dont chit him, ...bikos hi is a gipsi.

continued...

Clip, clop, clip, clop	Klip Klap Klip Klap
sound the hooves of the skinny horse,	saund de huvs of skini hors
for Mrs. Naiman at a good address,	for misis Naiman an gut adres
for old Sharkesi, the *primash*	for old Shrkezi, de primash
whose house is on the old city square,	vich haus is an siti skver.
O hurry up, a teacher is waiting	O heri ab, a ticherin is veiding
and she donates some coal scraps	and shi giv sam kol skreps
for the cold gypsy shack.	for kold gipsi shek.
For Judge Markovich, oh, he must be fast	For Gag Markovich, ou hi mas bi fest
just in case the police take him to jail.	gas in kes, if polismen tek him tu de gel.
For madam Panich,	For madam Panich
secretary in the town office	sekreteri in taun ofis
where the damn tax is due	ver dem teks is du
and no money is left for that	and no mani is left for det
at the end of the long day.	an end of det long dei.
Clip, clop, clip, clop	Klip Klap Klip Klap
sound the hoofs of the skinny horse	saund de huvs of skini hors
pulling old Vida, the coal deliverer	puling old Vida, de kol deliverer
with his little bottle of slivovitz	vit his lital badel of slivovic
huge chunk of bread	hjuch chank of bred
in which some sausage is hiding	in vich sosich is haiding
cheerfully taking new orders for coal	frenli teking nju orders of kol
from people who need his service	from pipel, det nid his srfes
right there, from his moving carriage.	rait der, from his muving kerich.

Croatia

The day I stopped bothering my dad—Dei ven I stap badering mai ded

Warm day spreads his white washing
through blue sky.
I'm on my way to the cemetery
my feet crushing saffron
in the green pasture, beside the train tracks
that passed through those hills.
Tired of fighting school bullies
of the steady beatings of my mother,
I want to run away from school and home
willing to join the gypsies
to wander from town to town
without any worries
without any chill.
Just want to say goodbye to dad
who stays in his grave
since we left him there
that stormy evening three years ago.

Day slowly grows older
losing his brightness
disturbed only by noisy trains,
certain bypassers that seeing me there
at the side of my father's grave
quickly whisper something in other ears.
Peace, nourished into birth,
makes me tired.

Then my mother shakes my neck
pulling me out of my dreams
starts beating me, as I scream, pushing me down
that mountain, beside the railroad
through the pasture of saffron
that hid now,
her anger stopped by no-one
only the amazed look of the train driver who,
unable to help a little boy
being mercilessly beaten all the way home,
protests with his whistle
in the first darkness of the cool night.

Vorm dei, spred his vait voshing
tru blu skai
An de vei tu simenteri
mai fit krashing safrans
in grin peshcher, bisait tren traks
det pesing dos hils.
Taet of faiting skul bulis
stedi bitings of mai mader
I van tu ran, evei from skul and hom
viling tu goin de gipsis
tu vander from taun tu taun
vit aut eni voris
vit aut eni cil.
Gast van tu sei gudbai tu ded
det stei in his grev
said vi left him der
det sturmi ivning tri jers ego.

Dei sloli gru older
lusing his braitnis
destrbt onli vit noizi trens
selten baipeser det siing mi der
an sait of mai faders grev
kvikli visper samting in dei irs.
Pis, nurisht ol brds
mek mi taet.

Den mader shuk mai nek
puling mi aut of mai drims
biting start, skrim, pushing mi daun
det maunten, bisaid de reilrod
tru de peshcher of safrans
det haid nau
her enger stap nouvan
onli amest lok draiver
anebelt tu help litel boi
det vos mrsenlos biten an de vei hom
protest vit his visel
in frst darknis, of kul nait.

Croatia

Sister Helena—Sister Helena

For her	For her
I never miss	I never mis
Sunday morning Mass	sandei morning Mes
or singing in the boring church chior	or singing in boring chrch kvaer
promise to be always honest	promis to bi olveis onest
even though I am a gypsy	iven I am gipsi
For her	For her
I wash myself daily	I vosh mai self deli
change my clothes	chench mai klos
from the little that I have	from des lital det I hev
never smoke or drink	never smok or drink
outside the gypsy camp	outsait as gipsi kemp
just to buy her favour	gast to bi her fever
For her	For her
I read poems	I rod poems
presenting them in the empty church	presenting dem in emnti chrch
below a crucified Messiah	belo as krucefaed mesias
who judges me for my sin	tu gag mi for mai sin
of loving one of His nuns	tu lav van of his nan
For her	For her
as I bring her daily stolen flowers	I bring deli stolen flauers
I cry in disbelief	I krai in desbeliv
seeing her from the church tower	siing her from chrch tauer
as she is fiercely kissing	ven shi kising firsli ...
in her rose garden	in her ros garden
our town's lord shepherd priest.	auer taun lord shepard

Croatia

Sunday when our cimbalo left—Sandei ven a cinbol left

Sad is the Sunday	Sed is de sandei
but then,... they all are	bad den, ... dei ol ar
in misery town	in miseri taun
of a Danube gypsy clan	of a Danjub gipsi klen
close to the road	klos tu rod,
and the train passing by	and tren pesing bai
in the flatness of Banat	in fletnis of Banat
Janoshi's old *cimbalo*	Janoshi old cinbol
is noisily loaded	is noizi lodet
on the pedlar's truck.	an pedlers trak.
To America it goes	For Amerika hi gos
when washed and restored	ven vosht end restort
to present our way of life.	tu present as laif.
Sad is the Sunday	Sed is de sandei
a day when we gypsies	a dei ven vi gipsis
see our miserable life,	si as mizeri laif
drink to our bad luck.	drink as bed lak.
Old *cimbalo* is leaving this gypsy town	Old cinbel living as mahala
and nobody gives a damn.	and noubadi giv a dem.
Instead, we gather	Insted vi geder
in little cold shacks	in lital kold sheks
with hardly any fire	vit hardli eni faer
yelling at each other	jaling an ichader
as our brains go numb.	ven as breins go namer.

continued...

Sad is that Sunday
somebody's kids are crying
and mother has only tobacco
to keep them quiet.
Why is nobody stopping the pedlar
his pants are down
in Milosava's shack.
The old Janoshi *cimbalo*
which stood in the chicken coop
when business was slow
so smelly and shitty
belongs to us!

Sad is that Sunday
rain settles in.
Somebody stole the widow's money
cold night swallows her tears.
Bora makes love to his wife
kids laughing, peeking through the door.
Old Svetlana in the shack beside
rubbing the back
of her toothless husband
hoping that she has better luck
than her sister, who married Janoshi
too many years ago to be remembered
in gypsy life.

Oh you damn Sunday
nobody cares for a *cimbalo*
in a happy pedlar's truck
that cost him nothing,
but twenty jars of cheap wine,
while he slowly puts in distance
on the muddy road.

North Serbia

Sed is det sandei
sambadis kidc are kraing
and mader hes onli tabeko
tu kip dem daun.
Vai noubadi staping pedler
his penc a daun
in Milosava shek.
De old Janoshi cinbel
vich stud in chiken kup
ven biznis vos lo
so smeli end shiti
belong tu as!

Sed is det sandei
reen setel in.
Sanbadi stol vidos mani
kold nait svolo her tirs.
Bora meks lav, tu his vaif
kidc lefing, ... piking tru de dor.
Old Svetlana, in shek bisaidet
rabing de bek
of her tutlos hasbend
hoping det shi hes beter lak
den her sister, det meri Janoshi
tumeni jers ego, ... tu bi remembert
in gipsi laif.

O ju dem sandei
noubadi ker for a cinbol
an hepi pedlers trak
det kost him nating,
bad tventi gar of chip vain
ven hi sloli keching a distanc
an madi rod.

Allah's storks—Ala storks

The storks nested once	Dei vos nesting vans
on the peak of the pale minaret	an pik of pel minaret
around which our poor roofs gathered	eraund vich as pur rufs gedert
there on the side	and der an de sait
where the gypsy *mahala* stood	gipsi malhala stud.
Clapping with their beaks	Kleping vid dei biks
when the *hoja* called	ven hoga vos koling
five times in the day	faif taim in dei
to prayer.	tu preer
The *hoja* hated them there	Hoga het dem der
but Allah wants them there.	Ala vans dem der
In a country where war stole everything	In kantri det vor stol evriting
kids watched, somtimes for hours,	kidc voch samtain for auers
the birds coming and going, clapping,	dei kaming and going, kleping
not having anything else to play with.	never heving nating als tu plei vit.
Every year, before they went to Istanbul	Evri jer, befor dei vent tu Stanbul
they flew around our minaret	dei flai eraund as minaret
to show us	tu sho as
how it is possible	hau is posibel
to live in peace	tu liv in pis
with neighbours and still prosper	vit neibers and stil prosp er
in this country of ours	in des kantri of auers.
Our *hoja*'s delight.	An Hogas dilait.
with Allah's blessing.	vit Ala blesing.

continued...

Those days
when summer returned,
thoughts of the last war and lost souls
nested in people's minds,
when winds roamed through broken houses
bitter because they were forgotten,
avoiding talking with the neighbours
especially those in the *mahala*
like they had done something wrong,
so many of them remembered the storks
whose nest now lay
below the bombed minaret
on the city square's cobblestones
beside the half-destroyed soldiers' lookout
that any strong wind could topple.

The storks came back once
stunned by the destruction
of that last war. They tried
to make a nest, didn't succeed
sadly accepting...
that Allah doesn't want them there.

Bosnia

Dos deis
ven samer retrn
tots over les vor and los sols
nest in pipels maind
ven vinds rom tru broken hausis
biter bikas dei vos fergoten
evoiding tok vit neibers
spesheli dos in mahala
laik dei danet samting vrong
so meni of dos remember storks
vich nest nau lai
belo bombt minaret
an siti skver, kabel stons
bisaid hef destroit, lok aut gamia
det eni stronger vind kut tapel.

Storks kam bek vans
staunt vit destrakshen
of det lect vor. Dei traet
tu mek a nest, ... diden seksidet
sedli akcepting, ...
det Ala dont vant dem der.

First love—Frst lav

That night	Des nait
winds promised fall	vins promised fol
to pluck all leaves	tu plak ol livs,
from old chestnut trees	from old chesnats tris
in our boulevard.	in as bulevard.
Rain came, to wash the city's cobbled streets	Reen kam, tu vosh sitis kabel strits
but then ran away	bad den ran evei
with the wind to play	vit vind tu plei
without finishing her chores	vit aut finishing her chors
leaving our city in a mess	living as siti in mes
facing grumpy day.	fesing granpi dei.
Running through our city,	Raning tru as siti
missing puddles,	mising padels
towards the cemetery I hurried,	tu vords simenteri I heri.
to tell my dad	Tu tel mai ded
before the coming night	befor kaming nait
dimmed all lights	dim ol laits
that a little gypsy	det a lital gipsi
with dark hair and eyes like coal	vit dark her and ais laik kol
promised to give me her heart	promis tu giv mi her hart
kissed me three times this evening	kis mi tri taim des ivning
when we were sharing,	ven vi vos shering
really, candies from the store.	rili, kendis from de stor.
Wondering if Dad could understand	Vandering, if ded kud andesten
so, in his grave	so, ... in his grev
that funny feeling	det fani filing
that made a guy like me	det mek gai laik mi
enjoy so much so miserable a day as today.	engoi det dei, so mizerabel, laik tu dei.

Croatia

Romany house—Romani haus

Our house	Auer haus
is built at the end	is bildet an end
of the little gypsy town	of lital gipsi taun
at one end	an van end
of the *Giorgio* town	of gorgio taun
with material from the dumpster	vit materijal from de dampster
one other end but still the end.	van ader end bad stil de end.
Without comforming to engineering plans	Vit aut konfort inginjering plens
for some reason still standing	for sam risen, stil stending
through all repressions	tru ol represhens
political upheavals	politikal abhivels
concentration camps	koncentreshen kemps
that almost got us all.	det olmos got as ol.
Our house is then	Auer haus is den
ends of all ends	ends of ol ends,
costing nothing	kosting nating
sheltering us all	shelter as ol
where we still drift, our own way	ver vi stil traivt, auer on vei
playing losers but still free	pleing lusers bad stil fri
to the *Giorgios'* surprise.	an gorgio soprais.

North Serbia

Rope Vendor—Rop vender

Drowned autumn leaves	Draunet otom livs
of all colours	of ol kolors
in a clear puddle on the street	in klir padel of de strit
glittering like golden coins	glitering, laik golden koins
on the firm breast of a married gypsy	an frm brest of merit gipsi
mirroring the colourful street vendors.	miroret kolorfol strit venders.
From the deformed sidewalk of the boulevard	From disformet saidvok of bulevard
(jolted once by an earthquake)	vich erdkvik goltet vans
in between the restored Muslim houses	in betvin restort muslim hausis
towards a little market	tu vord lital market
with *gamia* and cracked minaret	vit gamia and krekt minaret
from which the *hoja* doesn't call any more	from vich hoga dont koling eni mor
only birds, and Allah	onli brds and Ala
refuses to tear it down.	refjus tu ter him daun.
An old gypsy	An old gipsi
with many secrets	of meni sikrits
strong hands, wisdom of an owl	strong hends, ... vizdem of aul
a woman of hard voice	vumen of hard vois
flavoured with tobacco smoke	fleveret vit smok of tabako
selling on her billowing skirts	seling in her lafti skrt
ropes, for timid horses	rops, for timet horsis
stubborn mules, wild bulls	stabern mjul, vaild buls
blankets for a donkey saddle	blankets for a donki setel
never letting her little grandchild	never living her lital grenchaild
out of her mind and eye.	aut of hr ai.
With the season bedridden	Vit sisen bed riten
hiding only a few warm weeks	haiding onli fju vorm viks
beneath her ample bedcovers	belo her lofti bed kaver
cold snow that now nests	kold sno det nao nest
in mountain peaks	in maunten piks
will soon be flying around	sun bi flaing eraund
upper towns	aper tauns
keeping farmers at home	kiping farmers et hom
and she still does not have enough	and shi stil hev not inaf
to survive the winter.	tu sorvaiv de vinter

continued...

Worriedly checking
a group of black clouds
which like town rascals
roughhousing on the uneven roofs of the town
could burst at any moment
spoil her business
pushing crowds
towards the shops
in the narrow streets beside the market
where they feel safer.

Macedonia

Cheking vorit
grup of blek klauds
vich laik taun raskals
rafhausing an aniven rufs, of det taun
vich kud brst, at ani moment
spoilt her biznis
pushing krauds
tu vords shops
in nero strits, bisaid de gamia
ver dei fil sefer.

Gypsy horse—Gipsi hors

In first undecided snow	In frst andisaidet sno
that hovered restless	det havers restlos
unsure where to land	anshor ver tu lend
around the ruim of an old church	eraund de ruin of old chrch,
in which once those bound for the gulag	in vich vans dos baunt for gulak
prayed in their chains	prei in dei cheins
before passing the Urals,	befor pesing Ural
a family of gypsies found a refuge	femili of gipsi faund his refjug
to give their skinny horse, taken ill	tu giv dei skini hors det gon il
on the voyage in this cold weather,	an des vojeg, in des anjuzuali kold veter
some shelter.	sam shelter.
Horse, that for the little hope	Hors, ... det for lital hop
of a warm manger	of vorm menger
that always turns out to be open pasture	det olveis trn tu bi open pashcher
has pulled their wagon all his life.	pul det cherga ol his laif.
Finally collapsing	Faineli kolepsing
leaving the family stranded	living det femili strendet
while taking a shortcut	teking shortkat
through that mountain pass.	tru det maunten pes.
A fire was made	Faer is meid
to protect them from the coming blizzard,	tu protekt dem from kaming blizard
a fire so far from the next town that nobody noticed	faer so far from nekst taun det noubadi notest
seven frozen souls	seven frosen sol
and one dead gypsy horse.	and van ded gipsi hors.

Russia (Urals)

Scrap dealer—Skrap diler

Heavy parts of farmers' plows	*Hevi parts of farmers plau*
iron hooks to hang killed sows	*aern huks tu heng kilet sau*
frame of giorgio*'s baby wheeler*	*frem of gorgio bebi viler*
smashed outsides of kitchen cooler	*smeshet autsaid of a kichen kuler*
some abandoned pots and pans	*abendet pots and pens*
one quarter of Victorian fence	*van kvoter of Viktorian fenc*
end of someone's iron bed	*end of sambadis aern bed*
squashed frames of bicycles, painted red	*skvusht frem of an baisikals pentet red*
foot of garden table	*fut of garden teibel*
nails from big horse stable	*neils from big hors steibel*
insides of grandpa's easy chair	*insait of grenpas izi cher*
three heavy used shoes from some strong mare...	*tri hevi just hufs of sanbadis strong mer...*
Filthy Romany child on top the pile	Filti romani chaild an tape des pail
with his skinny father hauling	vich his skini fader holing
on its big wheels, a hand pulled wagon	an big vil, hand puld vegen
on the muddy road	an madi rod
to sell that beautiful scrap	tu sel det bjutifol skrep
just to make a living	gast tu mek a living
in the *Giorgio*'s rich town	in gorgio rich taun.

Belgium

Knife sharpener—Naif sharpener

His grinding stone
mounted on a little wooden cart
that he pushed around
knew every knife in the county.
Chisels, axes ... big or small
collections of drills,
gone dull turning in heavy wooden beams.
In bad times, when war was raging
even doctors needed his help
to sharpen their scalpels
cutting too many people's limbs.
Always taking a little money
never forgetting to be funny
giving a compliment or two
to every woman
(suitable to her age and status)
who'd brought a knife or two
to his travelling shop.
Sometimes fixing
pans and pots
just for a loaf of bread
(if money was short in the *Giorgio* town),
or a bowl of soup
by the family table, below a warm roof.
Reminding the old grandpa
that when he shaves again
the razor is sharp now
and could cost him his old neck.
Cheerfully advertising
his sharpening business
with his loud singing
through the cobbled streets
of our city.

His krainting ston
mauntet an lital vuden kar
det hi push eraund
nju evri naif in de kaunti.
Chisels, akses ... big or smol
kolekshen of drils,
gon dol trning in hevi vuden bims.
In bed taim, ven vors vos reging
iven doktors nid his help
tu sharpen dei opereshen naivs
kating tu meni of pipels limps.
Olveis teking smol mani
never ferget tu bi fani
giving kompliments or tu
tu evri vumen
akceptibel for her eg and status
vich brodet naif or tu
in his traveling shop.
Fiksing samtaim
pens and potc
gast for lof of bred
if mani vos short in gorgio town
or bol of sup
bei femili tebel, belo vorm ruf.
Remembering old grenpa
ven hi shev egen
det reser is sharp nau
and kud kost him his old nek.
Frenli advertaising
his sharpening bisnis
vit his laut singing
tru de kabel strits
of auer siti.

Romany stars—Romani stars

For every love	For evri lav
there is a happy family	der is a hepi femili
for every family	for evri femili
there is one wagon	der is van cherga
by every wagon	bai evri cherga
there is one camp fire	der is van kemp faer
from every fire	from evri faer
there are sparks flying up	der ar faer tingel
that gather in the lofty skirt of night	det geder, in de lofti skrt of a nait
turning in time into stars.	trning vit de taim, tu stars.
Whenever a new star	Ven ever de nju star
starts to twinkle in the dark sky	start tvinkel, in dark skai
a new gypsy fire is laid	a nju gipsi faer is led
beside the wagon	bai de cherga
letting all the people in the world know	lving ol pipel in de vorld no
that a new happy family	det nju hepi femili
cooks their first supper.	kuk her frst sapar.

Romania

Remembering our life—Remember auer laif

We were only twelve	Vi vos onli tvelf
when they made our marriage	ven dei mek as a merich
never asking us to agree on this matter	never asking as tu egri an des meter
and I kissed you before all the noisy guests	and I kis ju befor ol noisi gests
never before knowing you	never befor noing ju,
hoping that you, with your family	hoping det ju, ...vit jor femili
would go home tomorrow	go hom tumoro
and I could continue to play	and I kontinju tu plei
around the city bazaar	eraund siti bazar
begging from rich tourists like always before.	beging from rich turist laik olveis vos de fol befor.
Cuddling up to you with my drunken head	Kadeling tu ju vit mai dranket hed
on our first night	in auer frst nait
instead of making love to you	in sted tu mek lav tu ju,
after I danced most of the evening	after I denc mosli of ivning
with the girls from our town	vit de grls, from auer taun
instead of you, my bride.	den ju, mai brait.
Through all those years	Tru ol dos jers
when food was scarce	ven fud vos skert
roof was small	ruf vos smol
road was long	rod vos long
and our kids kept surprising us	and auer kidc kip sopraising as
arriving every year or so,	eraiving evri jer or so,
I was always leaving you with them	olveis living ju vit dem
sometimes never returned home for a year	samtaim never rodet hom for a jer
to save enough	tu sef inaf
to marry them all	tu meri dem ol
give them the same start	giv him sam start
so life has something to bite	so laif hes samting tu bait
before he hurts them.	befor hi hert dem.
You went with me, when grandchildren arrived	Ju ran vit mi, ven grenchildren eraivt
in the city's clean hospital.	in siti klin hospital.
We travelled back home to our village	Travel bek hom, tu auer mahala
in our good clothes, through the sky	in gud klos, tru de skai
arriving in a taxi at a just-purchased home	eraiving vit teksi in gast bodet hom
where all that count wealth	ver ol det kaunt vat
sit beside us, calling us sir and madam.	sitet bisaid as, koling as sr and misis.
Now we are old, hugging the heat of the stove	Nau vi ar old, haging de hit of stov
I am still in love with you	I am stil in lav vit ju
realizing how much I lost	rielaizing hau mach I lost
of you	of ju
when I was away from you	ven I vos evei from ju.

Macedonia

Satan Sara—Satan Sara

Her soul may never find peace	Her sol mei never faund de pis
for the awful things she's done	for ofol tinks shi dan
in her short life.	in her shortli laif.
With sixteen summers, and her beauty	Vit sikstin somer, ... and her bjuti
she was given to a rich fellow	shi vos given tu rich felo
who took her in good faith.	det tuk her in a gut feet.
The wedding was big	Merich vos big
and took a week to pass,	and nid a vik tu pes.
In the summers that followed	In samers det folo
no one could hear a child's cry	noubadi kud hiret a chailds krai
from the new shack that they built together.	from a njuli shek, det dei bild tugeder.
Soon fights were erupting	Sun faits erapting
from the previously quiet home	from privjes kvaet hom
taking more and more of each coming day.	teking mor and mor of ich kaming dei.
Next summer, working far from home	Nekst samer, vorking far from hom
her husband forgot to return,	her hasbent ferget tu retrn,
leaving the gossips to tell her	living gosop tu tel her
that he was living with some other	det hi liv, ... vit sam ader
who gave him a child.	det giv him a chald.
Soon she felt the town's laughter	Sun shi fel an tauns lefter
just because she could not bear a baby.	gast bikos shi kud not ber a bebi.
"You are cursed,"	Ju a krsed,
and they would pull their kids away from her,	dei pul dei kidc evei from her.
believing she could bring bad luck.	beliving, shi kud bring a bed lak.
Girls who wanted to marry	Gerls det van tu meri
were told they should not be talking to her.	shud not bi toking tu her.
Years slowly faded away	Jers sloli fedet evei
she was still a beautiful girl	shi vos stil a bjutifol gerl
but lonely like a distant star	bad lonli laik a distant star
in the cool dark night.	in kul dark nait.
She spent her days	Shi spend her deis
hiding in her shack	haiding in her shek
enjoying nights sharing the narrow streets	engoing naits shering as nero strits
with the town dogs or local drunks	vit taun dogs or lokal dranks
who never harmed her,	det never harm her,
visited only by her friend	vizit onli from her fren
who could not help but	vich kud not help her
get pregnant, being a normal soul	geting pregnet, biing normal sol
but refused to give up	bad refjus tu giv ab
on her good friend	an gut fren
even when her husband ordered her.	iven her hasbent order her.

continued...

On such a visit	Bai sacha vizit
Sara got the news from her friend	Sara god de njus from her fren
that her friend was once again in hope	det shi is vans egen in hop,
waiting for her fifth child.	veiding for fift chaild.
That was when Satan took Sara's mind	Den de Satan tuk Saras main
and soon Sara was proclaiming to all and sundry	sun prokleming tu ol kraud
that she was miraculouly	det shi is mirakelesli
for the first time in her life pregnant	for frst taim in her laif pregnet
ignoring the laughter of those souls	ignoring lefter, of ol sols
who didn't believe her at all	vich diden beliv her et ol.
proudly showing her big belly	praudli shoing her big beli
to everyone in the town.	tu evrivan in de taun.
But at the start of winter	Bad an start of a vinter
in her cold shack	in her kold shek
just hours before a big blizzard of snow	gast auers befor big sno blizard
talk ran around the little town	tuk ran an des lital taun
in disbelief the women gathered	in desbeliv vumens geder
to take a look, and heard the baby cry	tu tek a luk, ... and her de bebi krai
who was certainly not from a Gaja's seed.	det srtenli is not, Gajas sid
People wished her luck, sadly looking at her son	Pipel vish her lak, sedli luking an her san
who seemed to be slow to catch his life.	det simstu bi slo, tu kech his laif.
Then Sara's friend was found	Den Saras frend vos faund
in the bushes beside the water hole.	in bushes bisaid voter hol.
She lay in the snow, with a cut belly	shi lai in sno, vit kat beli
from which somebody had stolen her baby.	from vich sanbadi stol her bebi.
This is when we all understood	Frst den vi ol andestud
the tragedy that rolled into town	tragik det rol in taun
we had behaved wrong in this matter	as on vrong in des meter
which pushed Sara to lose her mind.	vich pusht Sara tu lus her main.
From then on, after she left	From den on, ven shi left
to live in prison	tu liv in prizen
and her friend was buried with her child	and her frend vos berit vit her chaid
and the shack where she dwelled was burnt	shek ver shi dvel vos brnt
so too all her belongings,	so tu ol her belonging
we all decided never to tease a woman	vi ol disaidet, never tizing a vumen
who could not have a child	vech kud not hev a bebi
just in case Satan	gast in kes de Satan
struck again.	strakt egen.

Bosnia-Herzegovina

Vigil for a gypsy town's guitar—Vigil tu gitara Gitana

sssssssshhshshshshsh	sssssssshhshshshshsh
Hot! Hot is the wind	Hot! ... hot iz de vind
that blows through our gypsy quarter	det blo tru as Gitanjera
hidden from the Gaja's village	haidet from Gajas vileg
and tourists' view	and turist vju
in a dry, narrow valley behind our church.	in drai, nero veli ... behain auer chrch.
Pablo's guitar was killed	Pablos gitara vos kilt
in a Gaja bar fight.	in Gajas bar fait.
Sadness is spreading fast	Sednis spreding fest, in betvin as
unrest is planned, then abandoned.	anrest is plent, ... den abendet.
O *patron* Carmen, why is it	O patrona Carmen, ... vai is det
that you have left here?	det vi hev tu liv hir?
Behind the old church	Behain jor old chrch
that is falling apart	det foling apart
its cheap bell, left here	vich chip bel, left hir
moves only on a stormy night	muvs onli in sturmi nait
to remember our unlucky roofs,	tu remember as an liki ruvs,
and our misery.	and auer mizeri.
sssssssshhshshshshsh	sssssssssshshshsh
Hot! Hot is the wind	Hot! ... hot is de vind
blowing through our *Gitanjera*	bloing tu as Gitanjera
to defeat our souls	tu defit as sols
to dry our tears	tu drai as tirs
the mother of our music	mader of auer mjusik
Pablo's old guitar is dead.	Pablos old gitara is ded.
On Sunday we gather	In sednis vi geder
for her vigil, in his shack	an her vigil, ... in his shek
not believing our eyes	not beliving as ais
the size of her wounds	an sais of her vunds
when a clean rag hides her steel eyes	ven klin reg haids her stel ais
when she is lying before us on the table	ven shi leing befor as an teibel
surrounded with our candles	soraundet vit auer kendels
and the wild cries of the women.	an histerikal krais of as vumen.
Oh, *patrona* Carmen,	O, ... Patrona KCarmen
shame should harm those people	shem shud harm dos pipel
for the bad deed they have done to us.	for bed dids dei dan tu as.
Pablo's guitar was his life	Pablos gitara vos as laif
now our tears fill her broken body.	nau auer tirs fil her broken bodi.

Spain

Turkish Bridge—Trkish brig

Relax. You are old	Releks, ... ju are old
built many centuries ago	bild meni senchuris ego
to serve the Almighty Sultan	tu srv Olmaiti Sultan
from Istanbul.	from Stanbul
Enjoy your peace	Engoi jor pis
be happy they didn't dismantle you	bi hepi dei diden desmental ju
only taking your river from you	teking onli jor river from ju
leaving you like a fool	living ju laik a ful
in the middle of a wet pasture	in midel of a vet pashcher
watching your river, which you crossed once,	voching jor river, vich ju kroset vans
protecting herds of geese	protekting hrds of goc
hiding flocks of birds	haid flak of brds
and this family of gypsies	and des femili of gipsis
in your cool gloom	in jor kul glum
ignoring town rascals when they horse around	ignoring taun raskals ven dei horsing
on your back	an jor bek
and keeping secrets of young lovers.	and kip sikrits of jang lavers.
Relax. You are old	Releks, ... ju are old
enjoy your life	engoi jor laif
In your days, peace was the last reason	In jor deis, pis vos letst risen
you were built	vaj ju vos bild.
They hated you then	Dei hetet ju den
you took our pride, our wealth,	ju tuk as praid, auer velt
our kids, stuffed on mules' saddles,	auer kidc, ... staft in mjuls satels
with guards on your ends	vit gards an jor ends
preventing crying mothers	proventing kraing maders
from following the caravan,	tu folo de karavan
bringing them back as janissaries	bringing dem bek als Janjichari
when they had forgotten	ven dei hev fergoten
that they were killing their own.	det dei kiling dei on.
It's your turn now	Is jor trn nau
to be good to us	tu bi gut tu as
you old grump	ju old gramp
built from our stones	bildet from auer stons
with our blood	vit as blad
from our taxes.	from auer teksis.
You are a good home	Ju ar gud hom
to this group of Romany	tu des grup of romani
thankful that you still exist.	tenkfol det ju egsist.

Bulgaria

Cursed Gypsy—Crsed gipsi

On early autumn days	In frst otom deis
when the old mighty Danube	ven de old maiti danjub
not used to the brisk winds	not just tu brisk vinds,
in his final rain	in his fainal ran
covered himself with a thick fog,	kavered him self, vit a tig fog
worried fishermen	vorid fishermens
again remembered the legend	vans egen remember legent
of a gypsy	of a gipsi
wandering through the swamps	vandering tru de svamps
around the mighty river.	eraund de maiti river.
In the thick smoke of a local bar	In tik smok of a lokal bar
when time slowly climbed	ven taim sloli klaimet
interrupted with heavy jokes	interaptet vit hevi goks
and slaps on the fat waitress's ass	a slep an fet veitreses es
in bits and pieces	in bits and pisis
from a gossip's mouth	from a gosop maut
a picture emerged of a woman	a pikcher emrg, ... of a vumen
with a crippled leg and a hump on her back	vit krsed lek and hanp an her bek.
"I'm telling you, brother	"I teling ju brader,
she was a lump of coal	shi vos lamp of kol
with a diamond,"	vit dajamond"
said the bony macho man.	Seid de boni macho men.
"Satan's body, with a Godly voice,"	"Satans badi, vit de godli vois"
said the other drunk,	seid de ader drank,
crossing himself across his huge chest	krosing himself, an hjuch chest
and finishing his drink.	ven finishing his drink.

continued...

She was a little girl	Shi vos a lital grl
from a musician clan	from musishen klen
on the Danube's upper run.	Danjub aper ran
Oh, could she sing,	O kud shi sing
pull laughter from every face	Pul lefter from evri fes.
every guest in a bar or at a Gaja's marriage	Evri gest, in bar or Gajas merich
enjoyed her voice.	engoi her vois.
But when her time came	Bat ven her taim kam
to be married,	tu bi merit,
her parents gave her	her perenc giv her
to an old coppersmith	tu an old capersmid
who had just lost	hu hes gast lost
his wife, the mother of five,	his vaif, ...mader of faiv
and a fortune in drinking.	and a forchin in drinking.
"Child, it is for the best.	"Chaild, ... it is for de best.
Your cursed leg won't be in the way	Jor krsed lek vont bi in de vei
if you are banging on copper all day."	if ju benging an de koper ol dei."
The marriage was a quick one	Mericch pes fest,
there was no need to spend a week	der ver no nid tu spen de vik
to entertain the guests.	tu intertein gast fju gests.
When the new day spread its white washing	Ven nju dei spred it vait voshing
over the blue spring sky	over blu spring skai
she was a woman, travelling in a noisy wagon	shi vos a vumen, traveling an noizi cherga
away from home, away from music.	evei from hom, evei from mjusik.
Hardly older than his biggest child	Hardli older den his bigeste chaild
she cooked and cleaned	shi kuked and klinet
worked the copper all day	vorket de kaper ol dei,
never complaining when she sat alone	never konplening,...ven shi set alon
beside the fire, in front of the bleak tent.	besaid de faer, in front of blek tent.
Travelling from town to town	Traveling from taun tu taun,...
gathering only abuse	gedering onli ebjus
from her drunk and lazy old husband.	from her drank and lezi old hasbent.

Then one autumn day	Den van otom dei
there, where the Danube touched	der, ver de danjub tachet
this little town, a fire arose	des litel taun, ... faer eros
taking the tent and wagon	teking de tent and cherga
of the hated old man.	of hetet old men.
When the first sould came to help	Ven a frst sols, cam tu help
they found the crying children. The man was dead.	dei faund kraing children, ... de men vos ded.
She had fled to the swamps	Shi hed fled in de svamps
taking nothing but her curse.	teking nating, ... bad her krs.
Soon after, fishermen claimed	Sun after fishermen klemed
to hear her haunting voice	tu hir her hanting vois
singing love songs that she remembered	singing lav songs, ... det shi remembert
as she walked through the swamps	ven shi vok tru de svomps
beside the foggy river where they worked.	bisaid de fogi river, ver dei vork.
"She punished those	"Shi panisht dos
that cheated on their wives	det chitet an her vaivs
calling them into treacherous bends	coling dem an trecheres bends
where their boats are lost	ver bots a lost
and the men are drowned,"	men a drauned"
mumbled the older man	manbelt de older men
still mourning his inlaws	det morning his inlo
whose bodies the river still hides.	vich bodi river stil haidet.
In the early hours	In erli auers
just past midnight	gast pes midnait
on a quiet night, under cover	kvaet nait, pul de kaver
of a thick fog,	of a tik fog,
the tired bartender locks his bar	taed bartender loks his bar
and all the drunks disperse slowly,	and als dranks desprs sloli
reminding him to say hello to his wife for them.	remaiding him tu grit his vaif
He leaves a plate of kitchen scraps	Hi livs a pleit of kichen skrebs
on his shop stairs,	an his shop sters,
just in case the cursed gypsy comes along,	gast if krsed gipsi kam elong,
then he takes the fat waitress to her home.	den hi tek a fet vetres tu her hom.

Romania

Night serenade—Nait sereneid

That starry night	Des stari nait
the moon scratched his belly	mun skrech his beli
on the shabby roofs of our huts	an da shebi rufs of aur hats
ignoring the dogs' barking	ignoring dogs barking
or the occasional cat fight in dark properties	or okezenli kat fait in dark propertis
where most of the souls were asleep.	ver mosli de sols ver a slip.
Through the empty streets	Tru de emti strits
the smell of late lilacs	smel of a let laileks
stretched through the warmth of summer,	streching tru vormt, of a samer.
when suddenly, beautiful music	ven sadenli, bjutifol mjusik
from a well-known violin	of a vel non vajolin
that played at the weddings of so many	det meri so meni
in our and the *Giorgio*'s towns,	in auer and Gorgio taun
slowly hovering in our gypsy town	sloli havering, tu as gipsi taun
teasing the ears of old and young,	tizing ers of old and jang
led us to wonder, what is the reason	let as vander, vot is de risen
for this unusual occasion?	tu des anjuzual okezen?
When we gathered, rubbing our eyes,	Ven vi geder, ... rabing auer ais
around the old *primash*'s house	eraund old primash haus
we found him, to our delight,	vi faund him, an auer delait
playing dressed only in his underpants	pleing onli, in his blesed anderpenc
a little bit drunk	a litelbet drank
to his fat wife of many years	tu his fet vaif, of meni jers
in the window of their house	in de vindo, of dei haus
in the company of two worried *gendarmes*	in kanpani of tu vorit gandarms
that were presenting her with a bundle of his clothes	det vil present her, vit his bandel of his klos
and a hefty bill from the town bar	and hefti bil from de taun bar
hoping for no trouble	hoping for no trobel
when she saw it.	from her sait.
The old fiddler, hoping to avert danger,	Old primash, ever from denger
hoping that she had forgotten	hoping, det shi ferget
all the times when he was late	ol his taim, ven hi vos let
spent all their money	spend ol mani,
on booze and honeys	an buz, ... and hanis
leaving her with big worries. how to feed	living her in big vori, hau tu fid
the kids from an empty soup pot	dei kidc from emti sup pot
and low kitchen fire,	an lo kichen faer
hoping that she could bail him out	hoping det shi kud bel im aut
because he didn't want to try out prison life	bikos prisen hi dont van tu trai
at least not tonight	endlis not tu nait
on her blessed birthday.	an her blesed brsdei.

Hungary

George—Gorg

In unwashed clothes	In anvosht klos
that have seen better days	det hev sam beter deis
with a fresh rose in his dishevled hat	vit a fresh ros in his shvivelt het
old vagabond...	old zitan ...
none other than gypsy George	non als gypsy Gorg
with his barrel organ	vit his berl orgen
and monkey Champagne	and manki Shanpein
brings laughter and music	bring lefter and mjusik
to our sleepy old block.	tu auer slipi old blok.
Songs...for people passing by	Shanson, ...for pipel pesing bai
songs of love...	song of lav
for a spinster on the third floor balcony	for spinstres an balkoni an trt flor
who stuff treats and a big cigar for George	hu stafs trits, and big cigar for Gorg
in the little monkey's purse	in lital manki prs
that just a minute ago was emptied...	det gast minit ego vos emtiet
down below.	daun belo.
He then goes up with breath-taking speed	Den gos ab, vit bred teking spid
climbing the rain pipe	klaiming de ren paip
to the mansard on the old saggy roof	tu mansard, an old segi ruf
to cheer up Chou Chou	tu chir ab Shushu
who never learned to talk or walk	det never lernt tu tok or vok
whose mother sticks some francs	vich mader stik sam frenks
in the little monkey's purse	in lital mankis prs
glad to see her daughter laugh.	gled tu si her doter lef.
Runs to the other ends of the house,	Ran tu di ader end of a haus
on the dangerour edge of the rain gutter	an dengeres eg of rengater
scaring pigeons into the sky.	skeriing pigen in de skai.
Soon it is all over	sun ol is over
at least until George's next visit.	andlis tu nekst Gorges vizit
Down the street, tourists follow them	Daun in de strit, turist folo dem
laughing and applauding by every house	lefing, and aplouding bai evri haus
where they stop	ver dei stap
forgetting the time, places that they want to see	fergeting dei taim, plesis det dei van tu si
giving all their little money	giving ol lital mani,
just for a special photo.	gast for speshel shat.
Poor Chou Chou stares across the window	Pur Shushu ster kros de vindo
at the pigeons that just returned.	an pigens det gast retrn.
The old spinster sinks in her roomy chair	Old spinsters sink in her rumi cher
behind the balcony flowers	bihain balkoni flauers
perhaps thinking over the moment just past	preheps tenking over taim det pest
then slowly, starts her needlework.	den sloli, start her nidel vork.

France

The storm that took my father away—De sturm det tuk mai fader evei

A grumpy morning	An granpi moning
unhappy	not hepi
after a breakfast of shadows,	after brekvest of shedos
walks through our city	voking tru auer siti
in the middle of canning season	in mitel of kening sisen
—bumping, in quiet streets,	banping in kvaet strits
into the smell of fresh pickles	vit de smel of fresh pikels
and new-made jams	and nju meid gems
which still sit in kitchen windows	det stil sit in kichen vindos
or quiet verandas to cool down —	or kvaet verandas, tu kul daun
happy that her shift will soon be over.	hepi det her shift bi sun over.
A lazy day ignores the wind	A lezi dei ignor de vind
and its cold tang	vich kold tang
exploring our neighbourhoods	eksploring auer neiberhuts.
pulling clouds into the sky	puling klauds in de skai
then when they group wildly bigger	den ven dei grup vird biger
they start to descend	dei start tu desend
like vultures smelling a feast	laik a gaers smeling a fist,
growing bolder, almost unstoppable	going bolger, olmost anstopebel
charging on the roofs,	charging an de rufs,
upper branches of trees.	aper branches of tris.
Joining with the wind	Goining vit det vind
that now throws down the ripe fruits	det nau troing daun raip fruts
from indifferent chestnut trees,	from indiferent chesnats tris
picks up a swirl of prematurely dead leaves	pik ab a sverl of primachur det livs
that had gathered in rain gutters,	det gedert bisaid reengaters,
blows the full washing lines	blo fol voshing lains
just to tease worried wives	gast tu tiz, vorid vaifs
who have started to gather in their washing.	det start tu geder dei voshings.
After a terrible night	After teribel nait
at my auntie's place	in mai enti ples
who never, not even in the height of summer	vich never, ... not iven in best samer
opens the windows	opening dei vindos
making the air in her bedroom unbreathable,	meking er in her bedrum anbridebal
my sister and I	mai sister and I
not understanding the sadness on all the people's faces	not andesten, sednis an ol pipel fesis
who surround us,	det soraund as
gathered in the hospital	geder in hospital
for the funeral procession,	for funeral proseshen
are staring in the face of the young "cursed" fellow	stering in fes of jang krset felo
his face full of pimples	fes fol of pinpels

continued...

who will carry the cross,	det leter keri kros
walking fast at first	voking frst fest
then waiting in the middle of the street	den veiding in mitel of a strit
for the gypsy musicians,	an gipsi muzishen,
and us, behind the black carriage	and as, behain de blek kerich
to catch up, before he moves again.	tu kech on, befor hi muv on egen.
Annoyed by the wind twisting his cross	Ernoit vit de vind det tvisting his kros
he keeps checking his distance	hi kip cheking his distanc
from the main group, somehow unsatisfied	tu de mein grup, samhau ansetisfai
with the distance.	vit de distanc.
The wind is picking up	Vind piking ab
pushing the gypsy music	pushing gipsi mjusik
and the crying of the hysterical women	and kraing of histerikal vimen
through the crowds of bystanders	tru krauds of baistender
towards the cold walls of	tu vords kold vols of
the German buildings gathered around the main drag.	kaiser bildings gedert eraund mein dreg.
Ushers it into big lofty entrances,	Asher her in big lofti entreces,
open windows full of people	open vindos fol of pipel
who watch us from a different level,	det voch as from diferent hait,
through the stairways,	tru de sterveis
tearing it apart on gargoyles teeth	tering her apart an gargoils tut
from which it emerges tortured	from ver shi emrgt torchert
passing through our ears	pesing tru auer irs
vibrating with the wooden angels	vibreting vit vuden engels
on this dusty carriage,	an des dasti kerich,
knocking on its glass doors	noking an her glas dors
and which riffs on, coughing shaking	in vich rifs an kofing sheking
falling almost unconscious	foling olmos ankonches
behind us, robbed of any rhythm,	bihaain as, robt of eni ritam,
hardly recognisable	hardli rekognaisebal
for those closer to the end	for dem kloser tu de end
of the funeral column.	of fineral kolon.
Like colourful mushrooms	Laik kolorfol mashrums
umbrellas appear,	amrelas apirt
having trouble keeping balanced	hevin trobel kip de balanc
in the strong wind	in a strong vind
after the first thunder.	after frst tanders.
Heavy drops pound us.	Hevi drops paunding an as.
The "cursed" man stops for a moment	Crset men stap, for a moment
then lowers his head,	den loert his hed,
gripping the cross harder, continues,	griping kros harder kontinju
followed by gypsies and the carriage	foloet bai gipsis and kerich
at a dangerously close distance.	an dengeresli klos distanc.
Rain annoying the musicians	Reen ernoing musishens

washing dust from the carriage roof and wheels	voshing det dast from kerich ruf and vils
making it more terrifying, unforgivable.	meking her mor terofaing, ... anfergivebel.
We walk beside our mother	Wi vok besaid auer mader
wondering why everybody is so sad	vandering vai evribodi is so sed
enduring her jerking and the iron grip of her fist	induring her jenking and aern grip of her fist
on our hands.	an auer hends.
For a while, the rain stops.	For a vail, reen staps.
The gypsies are playing loud sad melodies;	Gipsi pleing laut sed melodis
the coffin is lowered.	kofin is loert.
The cross carrier is attended to by his mother.	Kros kerier hev ol atenchen from his mader
Then the storm returns with a vengeance	den, sturm retrn vit venges
people running to hide.	pipel raning tu haid.
The gypsies play for a while, but then	Gipsis plei for a vail bad den
gather below the trees	gedert belo de tri,
to protect their instruments,	tu protekt dei instruments.
draining out their wooden bodies.	draing aut dei vuden bodis
In big lumps, a worker pushes on to the coffin	In big lamps vorker pushing an de kofin
earth that is turning slowly to mud	de erd det trning sloli tu mad
throwing all the wreaths on the little hill	troing ol dos rifs an de lital hil
that is already dissolving in the thick rain.	det desolving in tik reen
My sister cries, wants to run away	Mai sister krai, van tu ran evei
but she is jerked close.	bad shi vos jenkt tu stei.
I understand then that this storm has stolen my father.	I andestud den det des sturm stol mai fader.

Croatia

Chiko—Chiko

Hey,...you! ... yes, you	Hej ju! ... jes ju
playing the violin	vich plei de vajolin
at the end of the wing	an end of ving
of the airplane in which I travel	of eroplein in vich I travel
ignoring the enormous speed	ignoring enormes spid
passing through the clouds	pesing tru de klauds
winds that could sweep you down	vinds, ... det kud svep ju daun.
You, who've followed me from my cradle	Ju det folo mi from mai kredel
in that poor gypsy shack	in pur gipsi shek
that never knew any luxury	det never nju eni laksheri.
You, who never changed your clothes	Ju, hu never chench jor klos
never washed your gypsy sweat	never vosh jor gipsi svet
never changed your luck.	never chench jor luk,
don't you get tired	dont ju go taet
of following me around?	tu folo mi eraund?
Always remembering me	Olveis remember mi
and my original	an mai origent
family left behind	femili left bihain
that somehow believe	det samhau beliv
I am a rich uncle	I am onkel rich
from America	from Amerika
because I sleep in my own bed	bikos I slip in mai on bed
and room alone.	end rum alon
Look at you, your long grey hair	Luket ju, ... jor long grei her
unwashed in decades, with your old hat	anvosht in dekeids, vit old het
which was already falling apart when I was young,	foling apart oredi in mai jut taim
shoes that pretend to have a sole,	shus det protending tu hev a sol,
suit that was made	sud det vos meid
before World War Two	befor vorld vor tu
for the old town butcher	for old taun bucher
who was twice your size	tvaises jor sais
and who, if I could trust the town gossip	vich, ... if I kud trast gosop
loved gypsies: had a mistress in our village.	lav gipsis, ... hev mistres in auer vileg
Still perfect	Stil prfekt
at playing a violin—	tu plei a vajolin
why do you never complain	vai ju never konplein
about my lifestyle?	an mai laif stail?
Perhaps you'd enjoy it more,	Preheps ju bi engoinet mor

continued...

if I had stayed home, in our village	if I steet hom, in auer vileg
to build a little hut,	bild a lital hat
father a dozen kids,	fader dasent kidc
argue with my fat wife	argju vit mai fet vaif
over money or daily food	over mani, or deli fud
get drunk every Sunday	go drank evri sandei
play with my half-naked grandchildren	plei vit mai hef neket grenchildren
when they come in my shack	ven dei kam in mai shek
looking for me	luking for mi
in hope that I have some extra food	in hop det I hev sam ekstra fud
offering them nothing but my self	oferin dem nating bat mai self
watching them grow.	vochin dem gro.
If you wanted that, my loveable	If ju vanet det, mai lavebel
guardian angel	gardien egel
why didn't you stop me	vai ju diden stap mi
the day I left the village	an dei ven I left vileg
catching a ride to Germany?	keching raid for Germani?
Remember? You got on the bus first	Remember? ju enter de bas frs
already entertaining those fellows	interteining oredi dos felos
that shared the coach with me,	det sher vit mi koch
patiently waiting	peshentli veiding
while I gathered my courage.	ven I tek mai krich.
Aha, you old Rom,	Ha Ha, ... ju old Rom
perhaps you already knew	preheps ju njuet den oredi
my life would be constant running	mai laif bi konstant raning
away from home	evei from hom
away from poverty	evei from poberti
away from friends	evei from frens
away from loneliness.	evei from lonlinis
Aye Chiko, stick around	Ei Chiko, ... Stik eraund
for a while yet	for a vail jet
I still haven't found my peace	I stil diden faund mai pis
our fated journey is anything but smooth	auer lur bi eniting bad smud,
but ... all that you know already.	bad, ... ol det ju no oredi.

near Darva River on the Croatia/Hungary border

Two musicians—Tu muzishens

Two blind brothers	Tu blaind braders
two perfect musicians	tu prfekt muzishen
two hopefuls, for their miracle	tu hopfols, for dei mirikal
two believers in Saint Sara	tu beliver in Santa Sara
playing this evening, ... Dilaila	plein des ivning, ... Dilaila
Two children	Tu children
two young fellows	tu jang felos
who still share the mobile home	vich stil sher de mobalhom
with their mother	vit dei mader
waiting for her to take them to church	veiding an her tutek dem in chrch
to play before the gathered crowd.	tu plei befor gedert kraud.

France

Gypsy mother—Chergashi mader

The moon rests his old face	Mun rest his old fes
on the roof of an old wagon	an de ruf of old cherga
peeking through the holes	piking tru de hols
at the neatly patched belongings	tu nidli pekt belongings
of an older couple.,	of a older kapel,
smelling the fresh-made supper	smeling fresh meid saper
and camp fire	an kemp faer
sweet thistles in bloom	svit tisel in de blum
around her camp, beside the road	eraund her kemp, besaid de rod
close to a river	klos tu a river
with trains passing by	vit trein pesing bai
just outside of the Gaja town.	gast autsait of Gaja taun.
She is waiting there, sitting on a log	Shi veiding der, siting an log
that the river brought her	det river brot her
from his travels	from his travels
hugging the warmth of her fire	haging vormt of her faer
with old bony hands.	vit old boni hends.
Feeling the warmth, her skinny fingers	Filing vormt her skini fingers
venture out of the sleeves of the red sweater	vencher aut of her red sveter slivs
that she wears only on special occasions.	det shi ver onli an speshel okezen.
Muzzling her joy	Mazeling her goi
deep in her soul	dip in her sol,
she seems to be indifferent	shi sims tu bi indiferent
covering her feeling, just in case that	kavering her filings, gast in kes det
...well, he might not show up	vel, ... hi mei not sho ab.
Her son, after thirty years of life-journey away	Her san, ... after trti jers of lur
thirty years of her not knowing where he is,	trti jers of not noing ver hi is
is coming home.	kaming hom.

continued...

Will she recognise him?
Hiding her rough face
in thick cigarette smoke,
somewhere below her over-sized scarf
she is contemplating whether everything is just right.
She is grey now,
sick of gypsy travails
ready to cradle in her hands
a grandchild or two,
even to settle down if a shack was provided.
Ignoring her sick husband
who lies in a bundle of rags
below their wagon
complaining over her supper,
an old man from whom life has taken every muscle,
every tooth from his mouth,
every desire to live much longer,
every hope that he could see his son once again.
Oh, how she is waiting
on him, who left when he was still a young lad.
Is he tall? Big around his chest?
Maybe he won't talk to her
who never went anywhere
never learned anything
has to trust the Gaja
who told her only that he will be coming to the town
supposedly this evening.
She trembles
waiting for the dogs to sense him
her son, who after a lifetime
is coming home
from America.

Kud shi rekognais him?
Haiding her raf fes
in tik cigaret smok
samver belo oversais skarf
shi kontenpleting, if evriting is gast rait.
Shi is grei nau
sik of gipsi travel
redi tu kredl, in her hends
grendchaild or tu,
iven setel daun, ... if shek bi provaidet.
Ignoring her sik hasbent
det lei in det bundel of regs
belo de cherga
konplening over her sapar.
old men, vich laif tuket evri masel
evri tut from his maut
evri vil tu liv mach longer
evri hop det hi kud si im ...vans egen
Ouu hau shi veiding
an him, ... det laik jang led vos gon.
Is hi tol, ... big eraun his chest?
Meibi hi vont tok tu her
det never vent eniver
never lern eniting
hev tu trast Gaja
vich tel her onli hi bi kaming in des taun
soposentli des ivning.
Shi tremling
veiding det dog senc him
her san, ... det after laif taim
kaming hom
from Amerika.

Romania

Spoon maker—Spun meker

In unsure snow	In anshor sno
down in a steep valley	daun in stip veli
a little city is shivering	litel siti is shivering
hugging an old Turkish *gamia*.	haging old trkish gamia.
He stayed too long in the market	Hi stei tu long an de market
all the way to the third call of the *hoja*.	olovei tu trd kol of hoga.
Ten — for a lousy leaf,	Ten, ... for a lausi Lev
a real bargain, in old time	a rili bargen, ... in old taim
and nobody even asks for his wooden spoons.	and noubadi iven ask, for his vuden spuns.
Now, in the freezing wind	Nau, in frizing vind
with his shabby clothes	vit his shebi klos
shoes unfit for his hike	anverdi shus, for his haik
no medicine for his child	no medicin for his chaild
with these damned plastic bags	vit des dem plastik beg
full of his unsold wooden ware	fol of his ansolt vuden ver
and no promised cough syrup	and no promiset kofing sirup
for his quiet wife	for his kvaet vaif
who has coughed blood for years now	det kof blad, ... for jers nau
at her young age.	in her jang eg.
He wants to beat the coming blizzard	Hi vant tu bit a kaming blizard
with the unsure steps	vit anshor steps
of a hungy man	of a hangri men
who ate nothing	det diden it nating
since he left his gypsy shack.	sait hi left his gipsi shek.
If he's lucky, he could reach his home	If laki, ... hi kud rich hom
just past that mountain peak	gast pest det maunten pik
by late evening,	bai let ivning,
but that damned blizzard slows him down	bad det dem blisard slo him daun
makes it impossible to distinguish	mek inposibel tu destingvisht
snowback from hard rock.	sno benk from hard rok.
Instead of walking up, he tumbles down	Tanbeling daun, in sted tu vok ab,
in a steep crevasse, when night	in dip krevas, ven nait
has inhaled all of the light.	inhel ol of lait.
He found his peace	Hi faund his pis,
just ... for an hour or so	gast, ...for auer or ....so
so the worst of the blizzard could pass...	ven vors of blisard, shud pes.
Warmth slowly ebbs from his exhausted body	Vormt sloli veg, tru his egsostet bodi
covered with snow.	kaveret vit sno.
In his cold hand, the empty torn plastic bag	In his kold hend, emti toren plastik beg
which had lost his spoons somewhere on this hike,	det lost his spuns samver an des haik
flips in the raging wind	flip in reging vind
above his stiff face.	tru his stif fes.

Bulgaria

Old herbalist—Old bilkar

His hot fire revealed every day	His hot faer revilt evri dei
of a long life spent in the mountains	of a long laif, spend in mauntens
looking for mushrooms, special flowers	luking for mashrum, ... speshel flauers
that the Gaja wants for his medicine	det Gaja nid for his medicin
delivered to the town.	delivert in de taun.
On his shrivelled face	An his svivelt fes
surrounded with long grey hair	soraundet vit long grei her
that reaches his shoulders	det rich his sholder
curling gently at the ends	krling gentli an de ends
in the shadow of an ancient hat	in shedo of an enchent het
hiding below in the twilight of	haiding belo in des tvailait
his bushy eyebrows	his bushi aibraus
two dark eyes are checking the visitor	tu dark ais cheking vizitor
in his gypsy camp	in his gipsi kemp
beside the small stream, on this lonely road	bisaid de smol strim, an des lonli rod
splitting that lush forest in half.	spliting det lash forest in hef.
Calming down his barking dog	Kaming daun his barking dog
and spooked horses, beside his wagon	and spukt horsis, bisaid de cherga
with his slightly raised hand.	vit his slaitli rest hend.
He knew I was lost, hungry	Hi nju, ... I vos lost ... hangri
in need of warmth.	in nid of vormt.
Throwing heaps of gathered mushrooms	Troing hip of gedert mashrums
and some wild fruits	and sam vaild fruts
from the drying boards on his wagon	from draing bords an his cherga
into a large iron frying pan	in larg fraing pen.
With a big stick, turning some potatoes	vit a biger stik, trning sam potetos
on the side of his campfire	an sait of his kemp faer
and a large clay bowl	and larger bol of klei
in which there was probably a hedgehog hiding	in vich is probebli hechkog haiding
caught down below that mountain	kot daun belo det maunten
in somebody's orchard.	in sanbadis orched.
Hoping that all this delicious food	Hoping det ol des delishes fud
would be enough to please me	bi inaf tu plis mi
because I was younger and stronger than he was	bikos I am janger and stronger den hi is
and could take it all from him	and kud teket ol from him

in this mountain pass	an des maunten pes
far from friendly souls.	far from frenli sols.
As we ate dinner the moon showed up	Vi et de diner ven mun sho ab
teasing our dog a little	tising auer dog a litel
then apologising, took to the distance	den epologaising, tek a distanc
leaving only friendly stars	living onli frenli stars
for our company.	for auer konpani.
The old man admired my tent	Old men edmaer mai lait celt
but refused to try out	bad refjuses tu trai aut
anything that I owned	eniting det I ont
taking only chocolate	teking onli chokoled
because my cigarettes	bikos mai cigarets
were too light.	ver tu lait.
We didn't talk much	Vi diden tok mach
not knowing each other's tongue,	not noing ichaders tang
and seeing that the camera made him nervous	siing det kamera mek him nervis
I didn't even take his picture	diden teking not iven his pikcher
which I regret even to this day.	regreting des leter tu des dei.
On the next day, when we parted	An nekst dei, ven vi part
I left him my chocolate,	I left him mai chokolet
which he seemed to like.	vot hi simstu laik
He stood with his old wagon	hi stud vit his old cherga
overlooking the entrance of that small town	overluking entrenc of det smol taun
that I couldn't reach yesterday,	det I kud not rich jestudei
giving the dog time	giving dog de taim
to escort me to the first line of houses.	tu eskort mi tu frst lain of a hausis.
Never said much,	Never sed mach
only lifted his hand lightly	onli lifting his hend laitli
if I stopped, as insurance	if I stap, ... als inshuranc
that everything was all right.	det evriting is orait.
Strange how that old man	Streng, ... hau det old men
in over-sized poor clothes	in oversais pur klos
could steal my heart	kud stil mai hart
doing practically nothing.	duing praktikli nating.

Romania

Ramiza of Arles—Ramiza of Arl

She is a little gypsy
barefoot ballerina,
below the indifferent wild chestnuts
and busy boulevards of Arles.
A clown, on cobbled streets
waltzing with an old toothless hobo
when the love business is slow
smiling at the amused crowd
picking her next client.

Posing for a bony street artist
in her little skirt, with big flowers
and three unmatched patches,
tired of making love to men with money.
Singing for crowds of tourists
some *chansons*, quickly gathering coins
that sometimes roll dangerously close
to the rain gutter.

Giving an early street cleaner a stolen rose
she politely bows like a noble lady
taking the neighbourhood dogs for a walk
hoping to find a drunken man
sleeping on a park bench
and his walletful of francs
pretending a balancing act
in the warm rain that catches her
with a broken umbrella and a stolen purse.

Promising good fortune
when looking in his palm
to the old unwashed vagabond
who gave her his best cigarette butt
and a deep sip of his holy cognac
which he never shared with anybody else.
He blushes somewhat when she kisses him
on his unwashed face as thanks for his help
when older men are rough on her
when men who just took her don't want to pay
or the town gendarme wants to catch her
to transport her
back to her old country
back to the Balkans.

Shi is lital gipsi
barfit balerina
belo indiferent vaild chesnac
an bizi bulevards of Arl.
A klaun, an kabel strits
volcing vit ol tutlos hobo
ven lav bisnis is slo
smailing an emjust kraud
piking her nekst klaent.

Pozing for boni strit artist
in her lital skrt, vit big flauers
and tri anmecht peches
taet tu mek a lav tu men vit mani.
Singing for krauds of turist
sam shanson, fest gedering koins
det samtaim roling, so klos
tu reen gater.

Giving erli strit kliner, stolen ros
shi polaitli bau, laik nobel ledi
teking neiberhuds dogs for a vok
hoping tu faund dranken men
sliping an de bench, in park
and his volet fol of franks
protending balansing akt
in vorm reen det kech her
vit broken amrela, and stolen prs.

Promising gud forchin
ven luking in his po
tu old anvosht vagabund
vich giv her best cigaret bat
and dip sip of his holi konjak
vich hi never sher vit noubadi als
Blashing samvat ven shi kis him
an his anshevt fes als tenks, for his help
ven older men a raf an her
ven men dei gast tuk her dont van tu pei
or taun zandarm van tu kech her
tu transport her
bek in her old kantri
bek tu Bolkan.

France

Mother—Mader

That old house	Det old haus
after thirty years of absence	after trti jers, of absenc
citadel full of security and dreams	citadel fol of sekjuriti and drims
from my past childhood years	from mai pest kidc jers
with the painted flowers	vit peintet flauers
which the soot of the open fire	vich sut of open faer
is slowly covering up	sloli kavering ab
leaving me only little hints	living mi onli litel remembers
hidden first, but later recognised	hiden frst, bad leter rekognais
worthwhile, like a fossil out of another time	vertfol, ...laik a fosils aut ader taim
from my life.	from mai laif.
My mother created them there	Mai mader kriet dem der
with a paint brush	vit a peint brash, meid from her har
to hide uneven walls	tu haid aniven vols
bring some colour	bring sam kolor
in unbearable poverty	in anberebal poberti
escape for a day, or	eskep for dei, ...or
until the paint ran out,	antil peint ran aut
the thousand reasons	tausend risens
why her life went wrong.	vai her laif vent vrong.
Her only son	Her onli san
the imprint of whose palms	vich inprint of his pos
one in red and one in blue	van in red and van in blu
are still there in the other corner of the shack	stil stend in ader korner of de shek
barely three feet high,	berli tri fit tol
who remembers the tickle of her brush	remember de tikl of her brash
before he touched the cold wall,	befor hi tach de kold vol,
went so far	vent so far
to forget his way back	tu ferget his vei bek
to that unworthy shack	tu det anvurdi shek
that, like it or not,	det, ... laiket or not
was my beginning.	vos mai begining.
Coming home with not much to show	Kaming hom, ... vit not mach tu sho
taking all these pictures of her	teking olveis pikcher of her
that she never really enjoyed,	det shi never rili engoet
preserving hastily in my fifties	presrving hestili in mai fiftis
the rest of her life, that I missed.	rests of her laif, ... det I miset
In long winter nights	In long vinter naits
beside the best fire that money can buy	bisaid de best faer det mani ken bai
when she can't sleep,	ven shi kuden slip
I read to her from the stash of letters	I rid her, from stesh of leters

continued...

never opened	never opened
neatly packed, in the order in which they came	nidli pekt, ... in order in vich dei kam
—some of them many years old	samov dem meni jers old
still hiding the paper money	stil haiding peper mani
I sent to make her life easier—	tu mek her laif isier,
putting the rest	puting de rest
back in the wooden box beneath her bed	bek in vuden boks, belo her bed
the biggest furniture	most bigeste frnech
in our shack	in as shek
beside the old German table	bisaid old kaiser teibel
and bare stool	and bar stul
which she carried	vich shi kerit
all the way from the city	olovei from de siti
many miles away.	meni mails evei.
That old shack	Des old shek
my home — why is it so hard	mai hom, ... vai is so hart
to admit the truth?	tu edmitet de trut?
Denouncing it	Denaucing,
would be like denouncing my mother	... bi laik denaunc mai mader
who made the shack from bits and pieces	det mek shek, from bitc and pisis
through all those years	tru ol dos jers,
so big once, when I was small	so big vans, ... ven I vos smol
treading behind her	troding behain her
asking for food	asking for fud
when she returned from begging	ven shi retrnet from beging
in the Gaja town	in Gaja taun
many miles away.	meni mails evei.
My home, like she,	Mai hom laik shi
has now shrunk, buried under the years,	nau srinkt, ... berit vit jers
memories of my father	memoris of fader
that died so soon,	det dai so sun
never leaving any photo	never liv eni foto
nothing to be remembered,	nating ... tu bi remembert
and yet I sense him here	and jet I senc dem hir
waiting for her	veiding an her
as she slowly but surely	ven shi sloli, bad shorli
loses her will to live.	luzing her vil tu liv.
Deep in the night	Dip in de nait

I am preparing her best skirt
in which she wants to be buried,
little pennies to throw into the open grave,
coins which will cover her eyes.
I must call the Gaja
to prepare her body
and burn all the furniture.
All of a sudden everything is so important:
is that bad conscience
or the wish not to make a mistake?
Standing in the middle of the shack
almost claustrophobic for a man my size,
watching through the dirty window,
in perfect silence,
the silvery beginning of a new day.
In a patch of thistles
close to our house
frost was hiding
scared of that night
who soon now would be packing it in,
who hadn't disclosed the stars,
had banned the moon from the sky.
A solitary wind stopped by, half asleep
to scratch his back
on our straw roof,
then went roaming somewhere else
where warm fires were already burning,
not waiting on the grumpy morning
that walked slowly, with puffy eyes
like a slut after a whoring night.
The house fire
cuddled below a blanket of embers
didn't want to be disturbed
sneezing if cold air
sneaked through the chimney
disturbing her peace
at the start of the sad day
which took my mother.

I prepering her lofti skrt
in vich shi laik tu bi berit
lital pnnies tu tro in open grev
koins vich shud kaver her ais.
I shud kol Gaja
tu preper her bodi
end brn ol frnach.
Olova saden evriting is so inportent
is det de bed konchencs
or vish, not meking mistek?
Stending in midel of a shek
olmost klostofobik for men mai sais.
voching tru drti vindo,
in prfekt sailenc
silveri begining, of a nju dei.
In pech of tisel
klos tu as haus
frost vos haiding
sker of nait
det sun bi peking in
vich diden dish de stars
bending mun from de skai.
A soliteri vind stap bai, ... hef a slip
tu skrech his bek
an auer stro ruf
den vent roming, ... samver als
ver vorm faers oredi brning
not veiding an granpi moning
det vok sloli, vit pafi ais
laik a slat, after huring nait.
Haus faer
kadel belo blanket of enbers
dont vant tu bi destrbt
sneching if kold er
snik tru de chimni
tu destrbt her pis
start of sed dei
vich tuk mai mader.

Croatia

Marriage deal—Merich dil

Since two days ago	Sait tu deis
when the gossip of the gypsy town	ven gosop of mahala
brought him the news,	brod him de njus
Reshad cannot find his peace.	Reshad ken not faund his pis.
Today shortly after his wife has left for work	Tu dei short after his vaif left for vork
he is weaving baskets	hi viving baskets
which no one has even ordered	vich noubadi iven order
in the time when he usually sleeps.	in taim ven hi juzuali slip.
The son of rich Ibrahim	San of rich Ibrahim
who has never made a dime in his life	vich never mek daim in his laif
but is known to the law, and prison too	bad iz non tu lo ... and prizen tu
wishes to make a deal for his little girl	vish tu mek a dil, an his lital grl Esma
who has just passed fourteen summers.	det gast pes fortin samer.
Refusing Ibrahim's boy would be impossible	Refjusing Ibrahims boi bi inposibel
if he doesn't want to shake the town	if hi dont van tu shek a taun
wants to still be a gypsy	or bi stil a gipsi
especially remembering the father's money	spesheli remembering his faders mani
lent when Reshad was opening his shop.	ven hi vos opening his shop
But to do nothing	Bad not tu du nating
could waste his girl's life	kud vest his grl laif
and all he can do	and ol vot hi ken du

continued...

is pray to Allah, swallow his madness	pre tu Ala, svolo his mednis
waiting on his damn wife	veiding an dem vaif
who is out reading palms	vich rid palms
somewhere in the Gaja town	samver in Gaja taun
instead of helping him	in sted tu help him
to solve this problem.	tu solv det problem.
All day he weaves	Hol dei hi viving
baskets that nobody ordered,	baskets det noubadi order,
scared to show his face in town	skert tu sho his fes in taun
or accidentally run	or eksidentli ran
into the rich father with his bad son,	in tu rich fader vit his bed san,
killing himself with smokes.	kiling him self vit smoks.
Surprised when the door suddenly opens	Sopraist ven dor vos open
letting fresh air flood his house	living fresh er tu flad his haus
Out of breath, a young fellow from a	Aut of bret, jang felo from
good coppersmith clan	gud kapersmit klen
with his father by his side	vit his fader an his sait
tired from running up the hill	taet from raning, egenc de hil

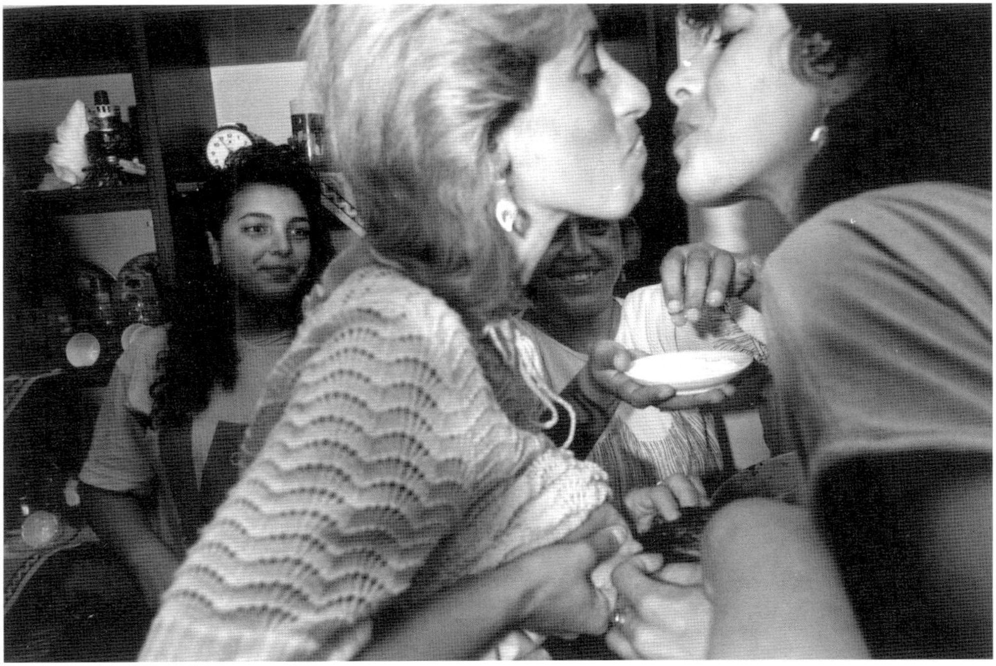

babbled quickly
so the whole neighborhood could hear,
“Is this a place where a beauty hides in a big basket?
If I ask her father for her hand
I will be happy soon
have a good wife
many sons and daughters
a long rich life
and grandchildren when the time is ripe.”

The old basket weaver Reshad
known as a good man, believer in Allah
swallows his smile
gives the young chap a long deep look
then comforts his exhausted father
so that the gossips don’t bite him
with rumours of his bad manners
Then, making a deal he didn’t ask for
with the old man
for a pot of money

abelt kvikli,
det ol neiberhut, kud hiret
Is det a ples, ver a bjuti is in big basket haiding?
If I ask de fader for her hend
I bi hepi sun
hev gud vaif
meni sans end doters
long rich laif
and grenchildren ven taim is raip

Old basket viver Reshad
non als gud men, beliver in Ala
svolo de smail
giv jang chep long , dip luk
den konfortet his egsostet fader
so det gosop dont bait him
vit rumers, of bed kolcher.
Den meking dil hi diden ask for
vit old men
for pot of mani

continued...

worried only when it was done
if his wife will approve of all that
when he tells her that a marriage will be soon
on the first night of the full moon
and the first of their daughters is taken.
Surprised somewhat, later that evening
that she totally agrees, which never was the case before,
without any complaints,
greeting the young fellow
to whom she had whispered the tip
about her Esma
down in the market
where she works.

vorit onli ven vos dan
if his vaif epruv ol det
ven hi tel her det merich bi sun
an frst nait vit big mun
and frst of dei doter is teken.
Sopraist samvat, leter des ivning
det shi totali egri, vich never vos de fol befor,
vit aut eni konpleins,
griting jang felo
tu vich shi visper de tip
ebaut her Esma
daun in de market
ver shi vork.

Macedonia

Two stones—Tu stons

Half a legend	Hef a legend
half a tale	hef a tel
I tell you what came to my ear.	I tel ju det, ... vot kam tu mai ir
Too many years before	tu meni jers befor
to know exactly the time,	tu no egsaktli de taim
in this town beside the Guadalquivir River	in des taun, besaid river Gvadalakvera
lived *señor* Pedro	liv senjor Pedro
gathering riches in olives and wheat	gedering richnis, in olivs and vit
stepping over every soul	steping over evri sol
that denied him his will.	det dinai him his vil
A bad harvest that year	Bed harvest det jer
took many by surprise;	tuket meni bai soprais
those that owed him money	dos dei on him a mani
lost their places.	lostet dei plats.
One of them asked him	Van of dem ask him
to delay for a day or two	tu delei for dei or tu
so his daughter could still marry	so his doter stil kud meri
at home, for her sake.	at hom, ... for her sek.
That evening when all the guests had gathered	Det ivning ven ol gest geder
Pedro and his men	Pedro and his men
threw everybody out	tro evribadi aut
torching the little place.	torchering a lital ples.
Walking on the shy narrow road	Voking an de shai nero rod
which tried to hide from the sad big man	vich trai tu haid from sed big mun
by hugging the stony hills,	haging stoni hils
listening to the cries of his daughter	lisening krais of his doter
he turned towards his house nearby,	hi trn tu vords his haus, in short distanc
still burning, in the valley,	stil brning, in de veli
and yelled, through the coolness of the night,	and jal, tru kulnis of nait
"Pedro, may you never	Pedro, ... mei ju never
have a marriage in your house	hev de merich, ... in jor haus
breaking your daughter's heart instead	breking befor jor doters hart
like you have just broken mine."	laik ju brek nau tu mai.
Sitting on his horse's back	Siting an his horses bek
Pedro laughed at him	Pedro lef at him
knowing that Lorena	noing det Lorena

continued...

was a beautiful girl, a good soul, loved in the town
and he was now the richest in the town
so, plenty of young guys
should be around when the time comes.
He never knew where the man went
who cursed his daughter and him,
never asked if he was still alive.
Sometimes he would give it a moment's thought
but his day grew too small
to finish all the jobs, so he worked... worked
and grew bigger, wondering why his daughter
even as beautiful as she was
never took notice of anyone's son
that could and would have married her
with great pride.
Finally, old Pedro
admitted in pain
that something had to be wrong,
paying priests and gossips
good money
to find out why she didn't want to be married
have a family and kids.

The whole town pitched in
to help the beautiful girl
knowing that she had lost her mother
at an early age
and had to live with her stubborn old father
from whom now even people from other towns

is an bjutifol grl, gut sol .... lavt in taun,
and hi is nau de richest in taun
so, ... plenti of jang gais
shud bi eraund, ... ven taim for des kam.
Hi never nju ver des men vent
vich krsed his doter and him
never ask if hi is stil a laif
samtaim, hi hev sam tots
bad his dei gro tu smol
tu finish ol gops, ...so hi vork ... vork
and go biger vandering vai his doter
iven so bjutifol als it is
never tek notis of noubadis san
det kud and vvvud meri her
vit big praid.
Faineli, old Pedro
edmitet in pein
det samting hes tu bi vrong,
peing prist and gosop
gud mani,
tu faind, vai shi dont van tu bi merit
hev femili and de kidc.

Ol taun, ... pinch in
tu help bjutifol grl
noing det shi lostet her mader
in erli eg
and hev tu liv vit stabern old fader
tu vich nau iven pipel from ader tauns

come to borrow money.	kam tu boro mani.
Soon they discovered	Sun dei diskaver
that the pride of the town,	det praid of dei taun
the daughter of Pedro, already had a lover	doter of Pedro hes oredi de laver
or at least, if the young gypsy Carmen	or so, ...If jang gipsi Karmen,
could call herself	kud kol her self
just that, Lorena's lover,	gast det, ... Lorenas laver
and the one who heard	and hu an erd,
freely told her angry father.	frili bi teling her med fader.
In the night that followed	In de nait det folo
the two were caught	der vos kot,
making love, just out of town	meking lav, gast aut of taun
where two big stones stand deep in the tricky river.	ver tu big stons ar dipt in triki river.
The cruelest judgements	Most krules gagment
about somebody's love	ebaut sanbadis lav
are given by people who themselves	givet pipel det dem self
have never learned to love.	never lrn tu lav.
Pedro himself	Pedro him self
beat up poor Carmen	bidet ab pur Karmen
banned all her family	bend ol her femili
from the town and country,	from taun and kantri,
that they should beg in some other country.	dei shud beg in sam ader kanri.
Hmmm — love is a castle	Hmmm, ... lav is kasel
in the clouds	in de klauds
and only those that share it	and onli dos dei sheret
know its dimensions, know the beauty of the place	no her dimenchen, no de bjuti of a ples
or the warmth that it can provide.	or vormt det shi kud provaid.
Lorena was left alone to cry	Lorena vos left alon, ... tu krai

continued...

refusing the priest and people;	refjusing prist and pipel
even living in the same house	iven living in de seim haus
she never talked to her father.	shi never tok tu her fader.
So many times	So meni taim
in the ruins of that little farmer's house	an ruins of det lital farmer haus
the old man sat, listening to how the wind's song	old men set, lisening hau de vind song
stripped of all words, filled the space	stript of ol vords, filing spes
in between the cold river	in betvin kold river
and the starry night above.	and stari nait ebav.
Watching how his trusty plot of olives	Voching hau his trsti plot of olivs
prayed for rain, but dark clouds	prei for rehen,... bad dark klauds
so close to their big crowns	so klos tu dei big krauns
saved the rain for washing the dusty hills	sevet, ... for voshing dasti hils
where long before that little devil had stood	ver long befor, det litel devel stud
who wished him bad luck.	vich vish him bed lak.
Hmmm — that land was maybe cursed	Hmm sam lend vos meibi krset
by our Lord, never produced anything	from auer lord, never produs nating
but gathering dust.	bad gedering dast.
A year passed, and nothing was done	Jer peset, nating vos dan
Carmen was back in town	Karmen is bek in taun
but no one had the heart to tell that	bad noubadi hev a hart tu tel det
to her father, to knowingly endanger good Lorena.	tu her fader, noingli indenger gud Lorena.
They were seeing each other at the same river bend	Dei siing ichader, ... an seim river bend
as before — scary, if you know old Pedro.	laik befor, ...skeri, if ju no old Pedro.
Then one evening	Den van ivning
gun shots were heard.	gan shts vos hert.
When the first olive pickers,	Ven frst oliv pikers

good loving souls, gathered	gud laving sols geder
at that river bend	an det river bend
just past the town	gast pest de taun
Carmen was dead, and Lorena	Karmen vos det, and Lorena
before her father could reach her	befor her fader kud rich her
had jumped into the tricky river	ganp in de triki river
where she drowned.	ver shi draun.
Hmmm, silver surface of the river	Hmmm, silver srfes of a river
divider of life and death,	divaider of laif and det,
deciding if somebody becomes an angel	disaiding if sanbadi bi engel
or enters hell.	or enter de hel.
To his death, Pedro watched those two stones	Tu his det, Pedro voch det tu stons
slowly understanding	sloli andestending
that the old river had no sorrows,	det ol river hev no soro,
they are dissolved	dei ar dezolvt
when they touch her waters	ven dei tach her votas
and washed to the sea.	and vosht tu de si.
In anger he died, defiant to the end.	In enger hi dai, feineli defidet.
These days, some people call those	Dos deis, sam pipel kol dos
huge boulders	hjuch bolders
Lorena and Carmen	Lorena and Karmen
still uneasy with that, I don't know why.	stil anisi vit det, I dont no vai.
Maybe this is the story's end.	Meibi des is de end.
Love is powerful	Lav is pauerfol
none of us could deny	nan of as kud dinai
her existence, prospers only if our minds	her egsistenc, prosper onli in auer mains
give her the right to prosper	giv her rait tu prosper
and takes from us	and tek from as
all rights to judge her.	ol rait tu gag her.

Spain

79
51
90

Gypsy Luck—Gipsi lak

Three times this evening	Tri taim des ivning
alerted by a siren	alert vit sairen
all the drunks, the waiter and the owner of a bar	ol dranks, veiter and oner of a bar
ran to the street	ran tu de strit
to protect the new car	tu protekt nju kar
of blessed Pan Frantishek	of bleset Pan Frantishek
that very good client of the establishment	det veri gut klaent, in det establishment
who once stole everything from city coffers	vich stol vans, evriting from Siti kofin
— what the little the Communists left us —	vot lital komjunist left as
falling from grace,	foling from de tron
making himself	meking him self,
a very rich man.	a veri rich men.
Three times, in this evening	Tri taim, an des ivning
every drunk, the old waiter	evri drank, old veiter
and the owner of a new bar too	and oner of a nju bar tu
returned empty-handed	retrnet emti hendet
having no clue who could be brave enough	heving no klu, hu kud bi brev inaf
to steal Frantishek's car,	tu stil de Frantishek kar
returning happily to a new round of beer	retrning hepili, tu nju raund of bir
some unknown numbers of plum brandies	sam anon nambers of brendi of plams
which the drunk owner of the car paid	vich drank oner of a kar, peet
for this crowd.	for des kraud.
When the siren sounds once again	Ven sairen saund vans egen
old drunks, tired waiter... and bar owner too	old dranks, taet veiter... and bar oner tu
heavy-footed, ... blurry-minded	hevi futet, ...bler in dei main
ran to catch a thief.	ran tu kech a tif.

continued...

Finding only a passing gypsy	Faiding onli pesing gipsi
with his collection of wooden spoons	vit his kolekshen of vuden spuns
trying to make a living	trai tu mek a living
selling from door to door,	seling from dor tu dor.
they beat him up, took his stuff	Dei bit him ab, tuk his staf
calling him names	koling him neims
banning him once and for all	bending him vans for ol
from selling on this street	tu vender an des strit
where Frantishek's car sits.	ver Frantishek kar sit.
Then happy to have taught him a lesson	Den hepi, tu tich him lesen
laughing, seeing him running	lefing, siing him raning
not understanding his bad luck	not andesten his bed lak
the sudden loss of his merchandise	saden los of his mrchendaisdei
they return to the bar	retrn tu bar
to toast, who knows how many times	tu tost, hu nos hau meni taim
to Pan Frantishek's car	an de Pan Frantishek kar
not knowing the neighbour's cat	not noing, det neibers ket
which loves to jump on the car to have a snooze	vich lav tu ganp an des kar, tu hev a snus
this lovely evening	des lavli ivning
triggered the badly adjusted alarm	triger bedli agastet alert
then, scared by the noise	den, skert from nois
and the stampede of drunks	and stanpid of de dranks
ran into the basement of the bar	ran in besment of a bar,
to hide.	tu haid.

Slovakia

Storks' revenge—Storks revench

Like old teeth	Laik old tus
the Gaja town lost all its ancient houses	Gaja taun los ol enchent hausis
that years before were the centre of a village	det jers befor vos center of a vileg
leaving only one	livet bat van
on the straw roof of which	an vich stro ruf
every year storks nested	evri jer stork ver nesting
always welcomed on their arrival	olveis volkom an dei eraivel
by the old folks	from old foks
who lived in that house all their lives	det liv inet ol dei laivs
waiting on their son	veiding an dei san
who forgot to return home	vich fergot tu retrn hom
from the Kaiser War.	from an kaiser vor.
When time had stolen	Ven taim stol
every year from their lives	evri jer from dei laivs
they died one late fall	dei dai van let fol
giving the Gajas and gypsies	giving Gajas and gipsi
little time to prepare a big funeral.	lital taim tu priper tu big finerals.
But when the sadness quieted down	Bad ven sednis kvaet daun,
the house was sold	det haus vos sold
to a strange man, grown rich years ago	tu streng men, gon rich befor his eg
by marrying a wealthy girl	bai meriing velti grl
with a crippled leg.	vit krsed lek.
Soon after they moved into the house	Sun after dei muv in des haus
gypsies were banned	gipsi vos ferbiden
from the family yard and house	from femili plot and haus
because he found his daughter	bikos hi faund his doter
kissing one of them	kisin van of dem,
from the gypsy village	from gipsi vileg,
on the squatter's land	an skvotert lend.
beside the river.	bisaid de river.
Then life returned to normal.	Den de laif retrn tu normal

continued...

When cheerful warm April
added to its flowers' perfumes
the smell of freshly plowed earth,
mother of the next harvest,
the storks returned.
Greeting each other and their nest,
wondering where the old folks were,
looking at the new owner
who was calling them a pest
instead of being happy to see them.
Choirs of frogs
kept the warm nights awake
in which the bloated moon teased
dogs, greeted new lovers
of the season,
wondering if the rich man's daughter
should kiss that young gypsy lover.

For a while
gossip nested below
the warm roofs of the Gaja town.
Then one evening, rapidly growing,
it burst from its hiding place
running down the street
whichpering in the bad man's ear,
"Your daughter has a lover,
and he is a gypsy ... ha, ha, ha!
They meet in the swamps beside the river
making you, old fool, the laughing stock
of this whole town where nobody likes you."

A new day smeared with the blood
of a slaughtered warm night,
quietly, ashamed of his acts,

An chirfol vorm april
eding tu his flauers parfjums
smel of fresh plaud erd
mader of nekst harvest
storks retrn.
Griting ichader an dei nest
vandering ver ar old foks
luking an nju oner,
vich koling dem a pest.
insted tu bi hepi tu si dem.
Kvaers of frogs
kip vorm naits evek
vich blodet mun tised
dogs, griting nju lavers
of a sison,
vandering if rich men doter
shud kis det jang gipsi laver.

For a vail
gosip nest belo
vorm rufs, of Gaja taun.
Den van ivning, rapidli groing
hi brst from haiding plesis
raning daun de strit
vispering in bed men ir:
Jor doter hev a laver,
and hi is a gipsi, ... ha ha ha.
Dei mit in svamps, besaid de river.
Living ju old ful, als lefing stak
for ol taun in vich noubadi laik ju.

Nju dei smirt vit de blad
of a slotert vorm nait
kvaetli, ... eshemt of hiiz duing

walked through the fields	voking tru de fils
where the next harvest was seeded	ver nekst harvest vos sidet
looking for a roaming wind	luking for roming vind
to cool his anger down.	tu kul his enger daun.
The crazy man	Krezi men
blinded with hate	blaindet vit het
waited in the bushes	veidet in bushes
beside the quiet channel of the river	bisaid kvaet chenal of a river
whose cold waters	vich kold voters
didn't want to be touched,	dont vant tu bi tacht,
in the first warmth of the morning,	in frst vormt of a moning
a disturbed fog waking up	destrbt fog veking ab
dragging her white skirt	dreging her vait skrt
through the cool forest	in kul forest
that drank from the river.	det drink from de river.

That tired man that nobody wants in the town,	Taet men det noubadi vans in taun
where gossips whisper always of his bad manners	gosop visper olveiz hiz bed meners
and the way he treats his family,	an femili tritment
waited in the bushes	veiding in de bushes
ignoring his wet shoes	ignoring his vet shus
and the cold that slowly crept inside his clothes.	and kold det sloli krip, in his klos.
Suddenly, meandering	Sadenli, miandering
in between the long grasses	in betvin long gras
and half-drowned willows, he heard her voice	hef draunt vilos, ... her vois is hert
mixed with the perfumes of spring	mikst vit parfjums of spring
too wait to fly, not revealing the place	tu vet tu flai, not reviling her ples
where she hid in this thick fog.	ver shi stei in des tik fog.
He started running	Hi start raning,
but soon abandoned the chase	bad sun ebendenet de ches
when storks which he disturbed in their feeding	ven storks, vich hi destrbt bai fiding
flew up, probably warning the lovers	flai ab ... probebli varnt dos dem lavers
who moved to a new hiding place	vich muv tu faund nju ples for haiding
from which no voice could touch his ear.	from vich no vois kud tach his ir.
His tired image floating in the still water	His taet imech floting an stel vota
of that dead channel, competing for space	of det ded chenel, konpiding for spes

continued...

with the fresh growing algae.	vit fresh groing grin.
Why did she never understand him?	Vai shi never andestud him?
He didn't love her mother,	Hi diden lav her mam,
giving his poor life	giving his pur laif
for a little gain, status in the town,	for a lital gein, ... stetus in taun
ignoring her crippled leg.	ignoring her krsed lek.
Then, once again, he heard them	Den vans egen, hi her dem
—somewhere there!	—samver der!
where the fog just lifted, in this clearing.	ver fog gast left, an des kliring.
But once again	Bad vans egen,
the storks flew up, disturbed in their works.	storks vos flaing, destrbt in dei voks.
Only the swathed grass	In svivelt gras
moulded to the shape of their bodies	moldet laik parts of dei bodis
spoke of their last hiding place.	sai of last ver haiding.
"Those storks — I'll kill them all!	Dem storks, ... I kil dem ol.
My daughter should never be with a gypsy lover,	Mai doter shud never bi gipsi laver.
will never be his wife!"	vil never bi his vaif.
Close to midday,	Klos tu midei
as saffron sucked the sun from the blue sky	safran sak de san, from de blu skai
storing sharpness in its seeds,	storing sharpnis in dei sids,
tired, he reached his home,	Taet hi rich his hom,
screaming and yelling	skriming and jaling,
pushing his daughter	pushing hiz doter
who had just arrived,	det gast eraivt,
throwing sticks toward the storks' nest.	troing stiks tu vord storks nest.
His wife knew her turn would be soon.	Hiz vaif njuet her trn bi sun.
Ignoring his swearing	Ignoring his svering
holding her tears	holding her tirs
for a time when she could cry them,	for taim, ven shi kud krai,
she wallked into the house,	shi voking in tu de haus
swish thump ... swish thump,	skvik tamp, ... skvik tamp
offering her crippled body	ofering her kripelt badi
to his attack.	tu his atek.
But instead, he climbed the roof	Bad insted, hi klaim de ruf
fighting the storks,	faiting vit storks,
then in a mad rage	den in med reg
he threw their chicks down into the yard	hi tro dei chiks daun in de jard,
shouting at the parents high in the sky.	shauting an dei perenc dip in de skai.
Worried neighbours gathered at the property fence	Vorit neibers gedert, an de properti fenc

taking the girl with them
commenting on the madness that they now
heard from inside the house.

There was no place
where the stories of this day
could be buried
so day gossiped with stunned night
just to keep his sanity.
Soon after, the worried night
slowly inhaled all the lights
cradling the nervous people
as they slept, listening full of goosebumps,
to what gossips expected from the angry storks,
when she saw this crazed man
in the early hours
leaving the town
to kill the gypsy lover of his daughter
—his daughter would be married in the village,
and only to a rich guy!

Young morning
sang to subdued day
its witnessing of the madman's fight
with the young fellow who stole his daughter's heart
down by the river.
Covered with blood, the gypsy fled
on an old wooden boat
floating down the river.

The crazed old man, screaming in his sickly glory,
walked home through the sleepy fields
and hurred to finish his crops
which were late now because of the lovers.
On the roads through the sunbaked fields
the steel heat of midday
was taking her dust bath
when he returned to the fields again,
leaving his house and wife
with a last reminder of who the law was.

teking grl vit dem,
komenting mednis det nau
in haus is hert.

Der is no ples
ver storis of des dei
kud bi berit
so dei gosoping vit stant nait
gat tu kip his seniti.
Sun after, vorit nait
sloli inhel ol laits
kredeling nerves pipel
in dei slip, lisening fol of gusbams
vot gosop akspekt from med storks,
ven shi so des krezi men
in erli auers
living de taun
tu kil de gipsi laver of his doter
in his vileg his doter bi merit
and rich gai onli.

Jang morning
sing tu sabdud dei
det vidnis med men fait
vit jang felo, det stol his doter hart
daun bai de river.
Kavert vit blad gipsi fli
an old vuden bot
daun de river hi floting.

Krezi old men skriming in his sikli glori
voking hom tru slipi filds
Hi heri tu finish his krops
hi is let nau , bekos dos lavers.
An san bekt filds rods
stel hit of midei
teking her dast bet,
ven hi vos retrning tu filds egen
living his haus and vaif
vit letc remeinder hu de lo is.

continued...

"It's over, o ye-es, I win!
That gypsy is gone
and the storks that protected him
they see what a crime against me gets them.
Yes, I win.
In a week or so
I'll break those two girls
and who knows, soon there will be a real marriage
in our house."

Back in the town
those two storks, still flying
like a bad omen
over the empty nest and their dead kids,
were joined now by others,
watched by gossips
aware of danger.

In the sticky heat,
not having had enough sleep
through the day that passed,
the mother and daughter
went to relax in the cooler house.

He is finished now
and will not bother them
for a while, and even the storks are gone.

"The storks are making revenge!"
yelled an old granny who was monitoring the sky
from her wooden bench by the door of her property,
but by the time she had gathered in her grandchild
to run for some help, fire
—carried in the stork's beaks
from a passing train some miles away—
had appeared, quickly spreading over the roof
nibbling around the house
looking with her fairy fingers for a good grip.
Excited now, she rose to her feet
blackening the sky

Is over, ... O jees, I vin
det gipsi is gon
and storks det protekt him
shud si vot kraim egenc mi, is laik
Jes, ... I vin.
In a vik or so,
I brek dos tu grls
and hu nos sun dei bi a rili merich
in auer haus.

Bek in taun
des tu storks, stil flaing
laik a bed omen
over emti nest, dei det kidc
goining nau from aders,
vocht from gosop
ever of denger.

In stiki hit
not heving inaf slips
tru de dei det pes
mader and doter
vent tu releks, in kuler haus.

Hi is finish nau
and bi not bader dem,
for a vail, iven storks a gon.

Storks mek revensh!
Jal an old greni det monitor de skai.
from her vuden bench, an properti dor;
bad in taim shi geder her grenchail
tu ran for sam help, faer
kerit in storks piks
from pesing trein sam mails evei,
apir, kvikli spreding over ruf
nibeling eraund haus.
luking vit her faeri fingers for gud grip.
Eksaitet nau, shi ros an hr fit,
blekening de skai

in which church bells were lost	in vich cherch bels vos lost
as they called the young people back to the town	koling jang pipel bek in taun
from the fields where they were working	from dei filds, ver dei vork
to fight the dreadful fire	tu fait det dretfol faer
before it could spread through the town.	befor shi spred tru des taun.
An angry day could only watch	An engri dei kud gast voch
the helpless old crowd	an helplos old kraud
that with pails wanted to stop the monster	det vit pels van tu stap det monster
who now stamped her feet	vich stenp nau vit her fit
on the old structure,	an old strakcher
knowing that somewhere in the house	noing det samver in de haus
lives were lost when it toppled.	laifs ar lost, ven shi tapel .

Up in the sky	Ab in de skai
the storks flew, almost amused	storks flai, olmos emjust
with the fire that they had planted.	vit faer det dei plenet.

Floating down the river	Floting daun de river
below the wooden bridge	belo de vuden brig
the daughter's wounded gypsy lover	doters vundet gipsi laver
stared into the white carpet	ster in vait karpet
of the pigeons' feathers	of a pigens feders
flying out of the bridge's gloom.	flaing aut at briges glum.
Instead of taking the boat on down the river	In sted of teking bot daun de river
he caught a ride on that soft carpet	hi kech de rait, an de soft karpet
with his sweetheart	vit his svithard
who was taking her old mother	Teking her old mader
for a heavenward ride.	for a hevenli raid.

From this time many years have passed.	From dos taim meni jers a pest.
The unloved man lives the life of a loner	Anlavt men liv laif of a loner
never changing the clothes	never chenching klos
in which always lurk a fart or two,	from vich olveis lerk fart or tu,
always hiding from storks	olveis haiding from storks
when they fly through the sky,	ven dei flai tru de skai,
minding any visit,	maiding eni vizit
tries to find his death	trai tu faund his det
but she always escapes in the crowd,	bad shi eskep olveis, in de kraud
taking somebody else instead	teking sambadi als insted
so he must suffer a little longer.	so hi kud safer litel longer.

Croatia

Romany blues—Romani blus

Remember in our our gypsy village	Remember, ...auer gitanjera
while the moon celebrated his birthday	ven mun celibret his brsdei
using stars like candles	juzing stars, laik a kendels
we promised our love	vi promis as lav
would last as long as our life is long	so long vi laif is long
Life is not easy	Laif is not izi
so many times we ended up lost	so meni taim vi ending ab lost
then like a ship from the high sea	den laik ship from hai si
we found ourselves a new place	vi faundet as self a nju ples
where we truly belonged.	ver vi truli belong.
You have left me now	Ju left mi nau
in a strange land, far from home	in streng lend, ... far from hom
at the end of my gypsy voyage	an end of mai gipsi vojeg
to watch the stars with some other	tu voch stars vit sam ader
and I am still wondering sometimes what went wrong.	stil tenking samtaim vot vent vrong.
Life is not easy	Laif is not izi
so many times we ended up lost	so meni taim vi ending ab lost
then like a ship from the high sea	den laik ship from hai si
we found ourselves a new place	vi faund as self a nju ples
where we truly belonged.	ver vi truli belong.

Germany

Screaming bridge—Skriming brig

In a little train station	An a lital trein steishen,
a short distance	short distanc
from the solid stone bridge	tu solid ston brig
built on a foggy stretch og the river	bildet an fogi strech of river
by an Austro-Hungarian Kaiser	from an Austro-Hangerian kaiser,
when spittoons were still in use,	vit spitun stil in jus,
with heavy planks, which were cooked in tar	vit hevi plenks, vich ver kuked in tar
before they ended up as the waiting room floor,	befor dei endet, as veiting rum flor,
and an old clock	an old klak
that survived two wars and an unknown number	det sorvaivt tu vors, and anon namber
of local revolutions still told the time	of lokal revolushens, stil tel de taim
staying patiently in his corner,	steing peshentli in his korner,
we waited for the next train.	vi veited an nekst trein.
Through the little window a mild evening was peeking	Tru de lital vindo, maild ivning piking
into the stuffy half-darkness	in stafi hef darknis
of the waiting room,	of a veiding rum,
bothered only by tired flies	badert onli, ... bai taerd flais
and the monotonous tick tock tick tock.	and monoton Tik Tak Tik Tak.
A fellow that was there already	A felo, ... det vos der oredi
in unwashed clothes, with an unwashed face	in anvosht klos, ... anshevt fes
sighing...smoking...twitching	saing, ... smoking, ... tviching
with his body...looking much older	vit his badi, ... luking mach older
than the years given him by our Lord,	den jers given tu him bai auer lord,
desperately tried to tell me his tale,	desperatli traid, tu tel mi his tel,
took a seat beside me	tuk a sid besaid mi
on the simple wooden bench	an simpel vuden bench
after getting the cold shoulder	after geding kold sholder
from the station clerk who ignored him	from ignorant steishen klerk
who had probably heard him so many times before	det hir him probebli so meni taim befor.
bored by now with his tale.	bort bai nau, vit his tel.

continued...

He lost his family, friends that he had,	Hi lost his femili, ... frens det hi hev
desperately needed a hug	desperatli nid a hag,
which I gave him	vich I gev him
being a good soul	biing de gud sol
to the fellow who has slept beside the railroad	tu felo det slip besaid des reilrod
for many years now	for meni jers nau
always trying to cross that bridge	olveis trai tu pes det brig
on that foggy stretch of river	an des fogi strech of river
always stopping short of touching the structure	olveis staping, short of taching des strakcher
watching others in disbelief	voching aders in desbeliv
when they walk to the other side	ven dei vok, tu ader sait
prays for them	prei for dem
the bridge is cursed	brig is krsed
too many souls sit all day in vigil	tu meni sols, sit an dei on vigil
in the muddy waters beside its feet	in madi votas bisaid his fit
the reasons and times they parted from us	iven risen and taim ven dei partet from as a
long forgotten	long fergoten
by those they left to die.	from dos dei liv tu dei.
Like some religious fanatic	Laik sam religes fanatiker
who in the busy town	det in bizi daun taun
warns people that the Lord is coming	vorning pipel, ... det lord is kaming
and, disappointed, realises	and disapointet riilais
that nobody cares,	det noubadi kers
he tells everybody his life's troubles	teling evri nju fes, his laifs trobel
details of his loner's existence,	diteils of his loners egsistenc
in an old Austro-Hungarian bunker	in old Astro-Hangerian banker
full of mice beside the entrance to the bridge,	fol of mais bisaid de entrenc tu de brig
which began many years ago.	vich start meni jrs ego.
From the thick cigarette smoke	From tik cigaret smok
where he hid his unwashed face	ver hi haiding, his anshevt fes
told how his life's story had become a legend,	tel, ... det in his laif ... trn tu legend
about a young woman, her five kids	ebaut jang vumen, hr faif kidc

on one autumn evening
when the fog hid that railroad bridge,
and this man, young then, drove the steam train,
watching through his window
in sheer horror, how five kids
and their mother
in a matter of seconds lost their lives
sleeping on the track he just passed,
and all that because her man left her
for a young gypsy
from a small village close by,
at least, that's what her crying mother told him.
Later in the year,
the gypsy that stole the young man's heart,
"surely a witch who has sold her soul to Satan",
gave birth to the young man's child
in the gloom of this bridge.

det van otom let ivning,
ven fet fog haid ... det reilrod brich
des men, den jang drov de stim trein.
Voching tru his vindo,
in shir horor, hau faiv kidc
and dei mader
in meter of sekends, lost dei laivs
sliping an trek det hi gast pes.
and ol det bekos her men left her
for jang gipsi
from smol vileg klos bai,
endlis des tel him den her kraing mader.
Leter in des jer
gipsi det stol jang men hart,
shorli a vich det sol her sol tu satan,
giv de brd tu his chaild
in glum of des brig.

Ha ha, he was not standing by
after he realised the death of his family
he left her, and she is roaming now through the world
The brunt of his hate, she is gone now.
Knowing that she is blamed for this tragedy
and probably never getting anything
in surrounding towns to raise the child,
she went to big cities
cut her connection to her gypsy town.

Ha Ha, hi vos not stending bai
after hi riilais, det of his femili
hi left her, ...roming nau tru de vorld.
den fol of het, shi is gon nau
Noing det shi is blemt for des tragedi
and probebli never get eniting
in soraunding tauns tu res de chaild
shi vent tu big sitis
kat her konekchen tu her gipsi taun.

Soon I left the man and his distracted world
feeling only sorry that I missed this gypsy
to give her a dollar or two
to make her and her child's lives somewhat easier.

Sun I left de men and his disytraktet vorld
filing onli sori, det I mis gipsi
tu giv her dolar or tu
tu mek her, and her chaild laifs samvat izier.

Croatia/Hungary border

Holy Mother the saviour—Mader Meri de sevjur

Wild winds licking	Vaild vinds liking
the scared faces of mountains	skart fesis of mauntens
over our heads	over auer heds
checking with its long tongues	cheking vit dei long tongs
side canyons that wander	said kanjons, det vandering
deeply through that mountain range.	dip tru det maunten reng.
Like a scared herd	Laik skeri herd
of hastily rounded-up sheep	of hestili raundet ship
clouds gathered	gedert klauds
blackening with their bulging bellies	blekening vit dei bolcht belis
the evening sky	evning skai
feeding on the shadows	fiding an auer shedos
of the hot summer day.	of hot samer dei.
The mountain road	An maunten rod,
was made more to please the mules	meid mor tu plis de mjuls
than the group of gypsy wagons	den grup of chergas
and especially my city car	espesheli mai siti kar
stuck somewhere in the middle of a canyon	stak samver in de midel of a kenjon
on the tail of this large group	in tel of des larg grup
on a warm evening that changes to night	vorm ivning, det chench tu nait
in a matter of an hour	in meter of auer
making all movements of utmost danger.	meking ol muvment altmos denger.
Sitting in my car	Siting in mai kar
I spotted the son, a young woman	I spatet sun, a jang vumen
and a dozen little guys	and dasent of lital gais
probably her flesh and blood	probebli, ... her flesh and blad
in unworthy clothes	in anvurdi klos
walking to my door	voking tu mai dors
enduring the first heavy drops	induring frst hevi drops,

continued...

calling me to join them
offering me the protection
of their saint, Mother Mary
that in the form of an enormous picture
stuck below the roof of the *cherga*
waited on our prayers —
"Holy Mother will save you."

When the tired sun
peeked through the gloom of the cold morning
unwilling to wake up the mountain tops
still sleeping in fog's blanket,
and our ears were slowly forgetting the thundering
of that sleepless night,
stuck in the road
just inches from my car
stood a new boulder
which had slid down, sometime through the night
while I was praying,
almost crashing my car.
Ignoring my missing watch
and pockets empty of change
I truly believed
before I parted from this happy family
that holy Mother Mary
had been our saviour.

Romania

coling mi tu goinem
ofering mi a protekshen
of dei sent, ... Mader Meri
det in form of enormes pikcher
stak belo ruf of dei cherga
veidet an as preer —
"Holy mader sevju."

Ven taet san
pik tru vet glum of kold morning
anviling tu vek ab de maunten taps
stil sliping in fogs blanket
auer irs sloli fergeting tanderings
from det sliplos nait,
stak in de vet rod
gast inches from mai kar
stud fresh bolder
vich slai daun, samver tru de nait
ven I vos preing
olmos krashing mai kar.
Ignoring mai mising voch
and emti pokets, from mai chench
I truli belivet
befor ai part from des hepi femili
in holi Mader Meri
de sevjur.

Bonnie the Romany's *rei*—Bonni de romani rei

You never saw a *cherga*	Ju never soet cherga
enjoyed the warmth of a gypsy campfire	engoet vormt of a gipsi kemp faer
that danced under the skirt of a dark night,	vikelt in skrt of dark nait
heard their songs.	hiret dei songs
You hide behind	Ju haid bihain
a stack of urgent letters	stak of nidli lreters
that arrived on my doorstep,	det eraiving an mai dorstep
always encouraging the gypsy cause	olveiz ekriching an "Gipsi Koz"
no matter what your life brings	no meter vot jor laif bring
so fragile it is.	so fregail laik et iz
You should be called a Roman *rei*	Romani rei ju shud bi
May Saint Sara, patron of gypsies	Mei Santa Sara, ...patrona of gipsis
show you your way	sho ju jor vei
and all your troubles always stop	and ol jor trobels, olveis stap
ten feet away.	ten fit evei.
Canada	

Chardash for a ballerina—Chardash for balerina

In the undecided light snow	In andisaidet lait sno
of a cold evening	of a kold ivning
so close to Christmas	so klos tu krismas
when most people	ven mosli pipel
stay home with hot toddies	stei hom bai hot todi
an old *primash*,	an old primash
new in this town	nju in des taun
like the music he plays,	laik a mjuzik hi plei
walks the streets in the low night traffic	vok de strit, vit lo nait trafik
beside quiet entrances	bisaid kvaet entrences
in the area where only the rich live,	in erija ver onli rich living,
with a bunch of roses,	vit a banch of roses
(bought in a hurry	(bot in de heri
before the supermarket closed for the night	befor supermarket klos for de nait
on a tip from his fat Marishka	an tip of his fet Marishka
good wife of many years	gud vaif of meni jers
who usually answers the phone)	det juzuali encer dei fon)
carrying his old violin	kering his old vajolin
that made him famous once.	det mek him femos vans.
Wondering how those	Vandering hau dei,
who called him on such short notice	det kol him an sacha short notes
so close to the festivities, knew of him	so klos tu festivitis, no dem,
and his music	and his mjusik
knowing that whoever they are	noing det, hu ever dei are
they are not of Central European descent.	dei ar not from central Jurop desent.
Down in the roomy entrance	Daun in rumi entrenc
of the huge house	of de hjuch haus
which he enters	vich hi enter
he is given a cup of tea	given kap of ti

continued...

to warm himself and his violin
then taken to the room
of a young ballerina.
He saw big pictures of her
when she was a star
dancing in big cities
enjoying rich audiences
before her fatal illness struck.
Accepting the red roses
that he has brought her
she impatiently waits for the first *chardash*
on her wish list
which she danced in an operetta
just before the bad news from her doctor.
The fiddler's music fills her room
where family and friends
listen too, happy to see her, after such a long time,
enjoying that music,
pushing the sad truth of her dying
if just for a moment,
out of their minds.

Chardash after chardash
slowly flooding the old house
trickling down in the basement
where the Latino maid is sitting
indifferent to this music
ready to serve at a moment's notice
anything that somebody desires.

tu vorm ab him self and his vajolin
teken tu dim rum
of a jang balerina
Hi so big pikchers of her
ven shi vos a star
dencing in big sitis
engoing rich audienc
befor her fetal ilnis strak.
Akcepting red rozis
det hi brot her
shi anpeshntli veid an frst chardash
an her vish list
vich shi denc in opereta
gast befor bed njus of her doktor.
Primashes mjuzik fil her rum
ver femili and her frends
lisen tu, hepi tu si her after sacha long taim
engoing det mjuzik,
pushing de sed trut of her daing
if gast for a moment
aut of der mains.

Chardash after chardash
sloli flading ol haus
trikeling daun in de besment
ver latino meid is siting
indiferent an des mjuzik
redi tu srv an short notes
eniting det sanbadi desaer.

Ignoring the stiffness	Ignoring de stifnis
of his fingers	of his fingers
some notes which went wrong	sam nots vich vent vrong
the old man plays	old men pleet
like seldom in his life	laik selden in his laif
tries to push	trai tu push
that ballerina's sickness away	det balerina signis, ...evei
—damn it, she is so young!	demet shi is so jang
Late this night	Let des nait
walking through the deep snow	voking tru de dip sno
he stops by the fence of the Gaja church	hi stap bai fenc of Gajas chrch
on the way home	an de vei hom,
asking the good Lord	asking gud lord
to take special care	tu tek speshel ker
of a little angel who just arrived	of a lital engel det gast eraivt,
giving Him a thousand reasons	giving him tausend risen
to be nice to her.	tu bi nais tu her.
Then taking a good sip of plum brandy	Den teking gud sip, from plam brendi
that hides deep in his jacket	det haidet dip in his poket
he troubles his old mind	hi trobeling his old main
walking home	voking hom,
with how he should explain	hau hi shud eksplein
this terrible loss	det teribal los
to his old wife	tu his old vaif
who probably, not even knowing the little girl,	det probibli, ... not iven noing lital grl
will cry all night.	krai ol nait.

Canada

Editor's Afterword

It is customary at Slipstream and River Books to include some comments from the editor who sponsored and prepared the book, and I am particularly glad to do so in the case of this remarkable collaboration of poems and photographs.

When Reg Silvester, judging the Edmonton Journal Literary Competition, discovered the remarkable storytelling of Croatian-Canadian Marijan Megla, he recognised the quality of this irrepressible writer who did not allow unfamiliarity with a new language to deter his writing. Megla creates his works in a written form of English based on the phonetics of his native language. Reg fondly dubbed these phonetics "Meglish", "translated" Megla's winning story into standard English, and encouraged Megla to gain the support of the Canada Council for the Arts for a book-length homolinguistic translation project which years later was published (in 1998) as *Vajolin/Violin*, a Slipstream Book from River Books, an imprint of The Books Collective. Like *Gypsy Messenger*, the book consisted of parallel texts, with the stories in Meglish and in standard English. Publishing texts special in form or content is the particular mandate of our Slipstream imprint, and Megla's work is a perfect example of the kind of book we love to develop. In 1999, *Vajolin/Violin* was shortlisted for the Writers Guild of Alberta Howard O'Hagen Award for Short Fiction, recognising the quality and innovation of this project. The book is now being translated into Croatian, and will soon be published in Megla's own language and home country.

Marijan is a working man, a pipefitter who spends a great deal of his working life building Canadian projects in Cuba. He has introduced scores of his colleagues to his literature by enthusiastically sharing his book with them. He is the very model of how universal an activity storytelling is, and how accessible the writing world can be to anyone motivated to create story. When Megla began to prepare this collection of poems, my office was enlivened by his frequent visits, and our consultations over Vietnamese lunches were lengthy and intense. During this time, Megla brought a celebratory feast to our office to share his excitement about his upcoming marriage, and over the years has introduced us to his adult son and now to his second family. Just the other week, he called from Cuba to share his joy at becoming a grandfather. Through working on these creative projects with Marijan, I have come to appreciate his *joie de vivre*, his loyalty and kindness, his fairness and his generosity of spirit. He makes the little dog who guards our office bark with his laughter, and then sooths her with his gentle affection as we work. There is never a dull moment with Marijan as a colleague and friend.

I have known Sima Khorrami for over twenty years, and I value her friendship as much as I do the visionary skills which she has contributed to many artistic projects in which we have both been involved. Sima is an Iranian-Canadian who took some of her art training in England. She is an extraordinary portraitist, documentary photographer, and printmaker, and has made a beautiful film about her heritage. "As a documentary photographer", Sima says, her highly textured and personal work "tends towards people on the periphery: street people, miners, the aged, burn survivors, assembly workers, prisoners, etc.—hidden people who have no voice, no face. Circumstances—natural, chosen, accidental—have placed them outside the accepted, expected ways of living in a modern industrialized world that promotes strongly narrow views on what it is to be normal."

Over all these years, one of her passions has been her stunningly realised documentary photography about Romany life. The first photograph in this book was taken in 1981, and over the years she has added to the *œuvre* whenever she could. On some of her travels in the early 1990s, she hired Marijan Megla as her interpreter and guide. Together, all over Europe, they sought out Romany people in villages and in *chergas* (caravans), in cities and in the countryside, happy and grieving, content and in distress, in daily life and in celebration, and Sima photographed them.

These were not always easy travels. In addition to the difficulties posed in finding Romany people and winning their trust, there was also the issue of the temperament of these two creative, intense and very different people. Suffice it to say that where Marijan is ebullient, Sima is reserved; where he is loud, she is quiet; where he is carefree, she is careful—but they are both equally stubborn! Their commentaries on their adventures would have expanded this book to twice its length, and perhaps someday those stories, too, will be written and published.

When we first began to form Megla's poems into a book, I knew that Sima's photographs would add immensely to the text, and convinced her to excerpt from her project these few photographs which relate particularly to the specific poems. Another book that waits to be published is the art book of the entire project, with the full range of her Romany images. I hope it will not be long in coming, as having been privy to a look through most of the collection, I can assure you that that there remains to be shown to the world a truly exceptional body of work. Simultaneous with the launch of this book, a photographic exhibition is planned which will display a further selection of these prints.

Meanwhile, Marijan continued to amass a stack of poems in a cubbyhole in my office, waiting for them to attain critical mass. Finally, the stack was thick enough and it was time to seek out an outside editor, another a River/Slipstream custom, which we follow to bring outside eyes to each project. Amber Hayward, a poet and novelist who has edited other poetry for us, "translated" about a third of these poems, providing invaluable sharpness of eye and ear, and pointed Marijan toward particular strengths. Because of the press of her own creative work, she shared this responsibility with me, and between us, we created the standard English "translations" you read here. These are usually completely literal to the Meglish text, the only exceptions being where an idiom or an elision in the Meglish creates a slight confusion on the page which it would not create when heard in Megla's own voice. There, slight changes have been made to keep both the clarity and the consistency of the poetic voice.

The last members of the creative team for *Gypsy Messenger* were: Jason Bartlett, who loves to typeset Meglish, he says, and who has created the design of both Marijan's books, with great effectiveness in harmonising the Meglish and standard English; Gerry Dotto, the brilliant designer whose cover design work with The Books Collective since its founding has been essential to the development of the River and Slipstream "looks"; and David Macpherson, who helped finish the production on a very tight deadline. T. J. Anderson and Miki Andrejevic have also helped with minor points of translation in the former case and liaison with the Croatian translator of *Vajolin/Violin* in the latter. Kim Lundquist and her colleagues at Priority Printing advised us on points of production.

Between us all, we have brought a particularly beautiful and interesting project to fruition. Now, at last, *Gypsy Messenger* is in your hands. You, the reader, are the last member of the creative team. Within the virtual reality of your imagination, Marijan Megla's stories, vignettes and lyrics of gypsy life and Sima Khorrami's superb photographic record have coalesced into something special, new, and unique. I hope you have had a wonderful journey through Romany culture and life as seen by Marijan and Sima, and that you have been enriched as I have by knowing the people who made this book—and the people depicted here.

Candas Jane Dorsey

Editor, Slipstream/River Books

Glossary

CHERGA – a Romany caravan or covered wagon, the original mobile home

CIMBALO – a musical instrument similar to a hammer dulcimer

CURSED – used idiomatically to mean crippled or mentally disabled

GAJA, GIORGIO – words used by Romany people in various areas of Europe to refer to non-gypsies

GITANA – gypsy woman (Spanish)

GITANJERA – gypsy village (Spanish)

LUR, or GYPSY LUR – the life-journey, the fated road, the travelled way of the Romany

MAHALA – gypsy village (Turkish)

PRIMASH – fiddler

REI, or ROMANY REI – a friend of the Romany, a *Gaja* who develops a special relationship of friendship and respect with Romany people

ROM, ROMANY – the real name of the so-called gypsy people; a person of that people

SLIVOVITZ – Balkan plum brandy (from Serbo-Croatian *sljivovica*)

Author Marijan Megla (far left), photographer Sima Khorrami (second from right) and two unidentified men photographed at a Romany circumcision celebration in Macedonia in 1991 during one of their research trips for the photographs and poems in this book.

Photo Credits

Frontispiece: Romania, 1992

Facing page 1: Gypsy chergas (wagons), 1992

Page 2: Gypsy woman, 1992

Page 6: Fortunetellers, France, 1991

Page 8: Portugal, 1994

Page 12: Romania, 1992

Page 14: Slovakia, 1992

Page 20: Romania, 1991

Page 22, 24: Morocco, 1994

Page 26: Bulgaria, 1992

Page 28: Iran, 1979

Page 30: Romania, 1992

Page 31: Romania, 1991

Page 32: 1992

Page 34: Croatia, 1991

Page 38: Bulgaria, 1991

Page 40: Madwoman, Spain, 1994

Page 44: Primash (fiddler), Romania, 1991

Page 46: Bulgaria, 1992

Page 48, 51: Gypsy Funeral, Romania 1991, led by "cursed [mentally disabled] man"

Page 52: Slovakia, 1992

Page 56, England, 1981

Page 62: Portugal, 1994

Page 64: Croatia, 1991

Page 68 -72: Marriage procession led by the groom-to-be's mother, carrying bride gifts, to the house of the bride, where the women anoint the bride's head with salt and breast milk from a lactating woman, for luck. In the last photo the bride is shown with her mother-in-law-to-be. Macedonia, 1991

Page 78: Slovakia, 1992

Page 81: Croatia, 1991

Page 82: Madman, 1991

Page 90: Romania, 1992

Page 92: Slovakia, 1992

Page 96: Romania, 1991

Page 100: Portugal, 1994

Author/Photographer photo: Macedonia, 1991